Fredd[i]
Ate My Hamster

Gabrielle Morris, 24, is a freelance journalist and a former owner of a stick insect called Charisma. Her writing has appeared in the *Guardian*, the *Sunday Times*, the *Mail on Sunday* and the *Yorkshire Post*.

Jonathan Margolis owns a dwarf lop-eared rabbit called Norman Hutchinson. He also writes for the *Sunday Times* among other publications, but is proudest of having been a Busy Bee – a member of the provisional wing of the PDSA – as a nine-year-old.

Also by Gabrielle Morris and Jonathan Margolis

THE COMMUTER'S TALE

THE BOOK OF LUVVIES

Freddie Starr Ate My Hamster

GABRIELLE MORRIS
And
JONATHAN MARGOLIS

ORION

An Orion Paperback

First published in Great Britain in 1994 by
Orion Books Ltd
Orion House, 5 Upper St Martin's Lane, London WC2H 9EA

Selection and editorial matter copyright © Gabrielle Morris and
Jonathan Margolis 1994

The right of Gabrielle Morris and Jonathan Margolis to be identified
as the authors of their own contributions to this work has been
asserted by them in accordance with the Copyright, Designs and
Patents Act 1988.

A CIP catalogue record for this book is available from the British
Library
ISBN 1 85797 914 1

Typeset by Deltatype Ltd, Ellesmere Port, Cheshire
Printed in Great Britain by
Clays Ltd, St. Ives Plc

For Toto, Tokyo's leading toilet manufacturers, for boldly going where no plumbing company has ever dared, in producing the world's first flush loo for cats.

Preface

ERNIE: What's that you've got there?

ERIC: A lobster.

ERNIE: A lobster? Are you taking it home for tea?

ERIC: No, it's had its tea. Now I'm taking it to the pictures.

(Eric Morecambe and Ernie Wise, *The Morecambe and Wise Joke Book*, 1979)

The front page headline in the *Sun* newspaper on 13 March 1986 announced in inch and a half high letters: FREDDIE STARR ATE MY HAMSTER. This astonishing assertion was made by a 23-year-old model called Lea La Salle, who claimed that the 40-year-old comic ate her pet between two slices of bread at her and her boyfriend's home in Cheshire. As might be expected, in the following weeks the story turned out to be slightly more complicated than it seemed. Mr Starr had not, of course, eaten anyone's hamster, but the story and headline became a modern journalistic legend.

Stories about pets liven up newspapers of every sort, from the *Sun* to the *New York Times*, they all carry them. Some pure black humour, like Mr Starr's alleged rodent activities. Others are in turn touching, intriguing and sometimes even a little sickening. They reflect, of course, the varied and unpredictable reactions of humans to animals – and vice versa. Sir Winston Churchill once said, 'Odd things, animals. All dogs look up to you. All cats look down at you. Only a pig looks at you as an equal.'

Sir Winston might have guessed that in the age of equality pigs would become household pets, as they did in the early 1990s with the advent of the Vietnamese pot-bellied pig, *the* fashionable pet of the day. But cats, dogs, goldfish and rabbits continue to be the mainstay of the pet-loving world ... and the mainstay of those preposterous pet paragraphs that keep newspapers from sounding too much like suicide notes.

We hope you enjoy reading this compendium of animal stories, which we have gathered from all over the globe, as much as we enjoyed compiling it. They give the lie to the idea that the British are the most animal-mad nation. America, France and Japan – especially Japan – have been a fertile source of daftness.

The Japanese almost lead the world in pampering their pets. Where else would you find a man teaching yoga to cats and dogs, or a leading plumbing company which makes a flush loo for cats? One leading Tokyo department store, Mitsukoshi, opened a new pet section recently. Normally pet departments are in a quiet corner or on a rooftop because of the noise and the pong. But not at Mitsukoshi. This store set its pet department slap bang in between swimwear and outdoor clothes sections. That is a measure of the Japanese fervour for fur and feather.

Not surprisingly, there are some wacky pet lovers in the USA too. In Tampa, Florida at one time, people who couldn't bear to have their pets buried had them freeze-dried instead. This meant that cats could maintain their life-like position curled up in front of the fire, whilst dogs could stand on eternal guard on the porch. Jeffrey Weber of Preservations Specialities Ltd hoped that humans would be next on the list for freeze drying, so that they could be displayed in glass coffins.

The French have become cat and dog mad. The romantic city of Paris boasts animal ambulances, specially designed to speed ailing pets to any of the 40 clinics that stay open 24 hours a day. One of these, the Klein Clinic, carries out about 100 operations a week, at up to £500 a time.

In Britain, we are prone to giving our pets especially silly gifts ... and special presents for pets at Christmas come with special price tags ... Why not invest in a miniature solid rosewood bed for your dog? Only £250. If your pooch is a pedigree, however, don't insult him by economising. Buy him the £350 four-poster from Harrods, or an upholstered chaise-longue for peke or pug to recline on. You may even care to splash out on the miniature waterbed – from £132 ... Or you may just prefer to read about it.

1
The Cat's Tale

Jessica and John Howkins from Headington, Oxford decided their 8-month-old tom-cat, Fluffy, was getting too smelly and would have to be taken for the chop. They spent £18.50 on the operation, only to find the odour lingering in the kitchen. They soon discovered the source of the pong – and the cause of Fluffy losing his tackle. John had dumped a bundle of smelly football kit in a corner ten days earlier and forgotten about it.

* * *

Alice Leeson, a 33-year-old New Yorker, took drastic action to stop her landlord evicting her cat Harry – she married it! The 5-year-old cat and his owner were joined in holy matrimony at a service attended by 30 guests. Alice thought that if Harry were her husband the landlord wouldn't be able to kick him out. In fact, if he tried, Alice was going to sue him. Oddly enough, her mother refused to attend the ceremony. She said that she couldn't bear to see her only daughter get married to a tom-cat.

*　　*　　*

Charlie the tabby cat got 80 feet up a pine tree before he realized that what goes up does not necessarily come down again. His rescue involved the RSPCA, the fire service, a tractor and a crane hoist. Three different people made it to within feet of the branch where Charlie was stuck, but had to turn back, defeated. Before Charlie was finally rescued, things became so desperate that an archer was employed to shoot a rescue rope up to the branch!

*　　*　　*

Jim Norman, a health club owner in Torquay,

kept having his car broken into. It turned out that passing animal lovers thought the fluffy white cat sitting on the back shelf, and looking decidedly glazed, was real. Jim tipped off police and RSPCA officials that the cat was, in fact, a rather fine model of his cat, Scampi.

* * *

In 1992, an exhibitor at the Tokyo International Fairground displayed toilets for cats. The product was designed by Toto Ltd, Japan's leading manufacturers of bathroom fixtures. The toilet, for simultaneous use by humans and their cats, was large and yellow and consisted of a single tank and two seats. One seat was standard-sized and the other was, naturally, slightly smaller. To make it quite clear which loo was which, a small plastic fish had been attached to the flush handle of the smaller model. The concept behind this extraordinary duo-loo was that you and your moggie could share that most intimate of moments together. Afterwards, either one of you could flush and all waste would go down the same drain. It took a team of designers 6 months and Y700,000 to perfect the loo, although it may never go on sale. Hirokazu

Tanaka, one of the designers, admitted that their original thought was that humans and cats should not use the same seats for reasons of hygiene. To add an element of credibility to the idea, Tanaka cited a video entitled *Professor Rocky's Toilet Training*, which was entirely devoted to getting cats to emulate humans when it came to toilet time. The toilet had not, at the time of writing, been tested on a real cat, neither was the firm thinking of producing a similar loo for dogs. Tanaka explained, 'Dogs are less intelligent than cats. We don't think dogs could do this.' Yasuo Kotayashi, who was visiting the exhibition, didn't think his own cat, Miiko, could use the loo. 'Our cat needs to scratch and dig after he's done,' he said. 'I don't think he's ready for this.' The only positive aspect of a double loo is that you can always blame any unsavoury smells on the cat!

*   *   *

Firemen in Southampton used all their powers of purrs-uasion when a moggie who was stuck 45 feet up a tree refused to come down. After all attempts to coax the cat down failed, the fireman turned a hose on it. Tiddles came down in record time!

*   *   *

When a family in Bromley, Kent took their tom-cat to be castrated, the vet did a double-take and asked to examine the animal a little more closely. Thinking he had some particularly absent-minded owners on his hands, he explained that he had already castrated the cat 2 weeks previously, and that, even if he was still misbehaving, repeating the operation would solve nothing. It turned out that 2 families thought they owned the same cat! He had been living a complete double life, eating, sleeping and purring in 2 homes. The cat was reported to be embarrassed by the discovery of this subterfuge, but relieved that he didn't have to go under the knife a second time.

*   *   *

King, a Siamese cat, was fascinated by the electronic toy goldfish her owner had bought in Hong Kong and put in a bowl at their Tel Aviv flat for a joke. King watched the mechanical fish whirr around the bowl until he could stand it no more, and swallowed it. He had to have an emergency operation to remove the fish – which was still whirring and bleeping inside him.

* * *

Staff at Tokyo's giant Shibuya Station were asked to hunt for a fat cat that sat on a mat – and delayed suburban services. The cat had been lounging on special sensor mats laid along the tracks to trip alarms if passengers accidentally fell off a platform. Twelve passengers had recently done so and one had been killed. But only a few days after the mats were installed, the alarms started going off without any apparent reason. The phantom feline of Shibuya – a well-built one, heavy enough to set off the alarms – was blamed, but never found.

* * *

An American found his wife's obsession for cats just too much. He hit her with one and then rubbed her face in its fish supper. He ended up in court.

* * *

The case of a cat a little untypically rescuing a stricken fish was reported in Des Moines, Iowa. A family's house had burned down, and the children begged firefighters to go into the smouldering remains to save their fish. Just as the men had agreed, the cat streaked into the house and came out with the goldfish held gently in her mouth. Sadly, the fish was already dead – from the effects of the fire.

*   *   *

In 1983, British national news was over-shadowed by the fate of a ginger cat. For two entire days, news reports faithfully informed the public of developments in the case of the cat which was stuck up a 150-foot mill chimney in Bolton. Steeplejack extraordinaire Fred Dibnah was called, and for two days he battled to rescue the cat. Eventually, a cat-lover risked life and limb, shinned up a creaky old ladder and grabbed the creature to safety.

*   *   *

Why should puss be content to play with an old boot when she could play with ... an astrakhan-covered musical roller, a clockwork rat, complete with black ears and pink eyes, a furry grey velvet mouse packed with a reviving tonic or a toy mouse covered with real mouse fur? All available at one New York pet shop.

* * *

For clever creatures, cats get lost more often than you might expect. Dr Matthew Dyer-Fane was so intent on getting his missing mog Fred back into the family home that he enlisted his 2,500 patients to help him. The doc would get up at 5.30 a.m. before his surgery to walk the streets of south London looking for Fred. When all else failed, he enlisted the help of a medium to see if she could trace the missing cat.

* * *

Skinny Ribs the Cambridge cat was positively averse to being found. When the one-eyed errant feline had been delivered to its owner, Mrs Francesca Christen, it stayed just long enough to devour a plate of best steak before disappearing off again. Thomas Dughery, a local pensioner, eventually found the by now not-so-Skinny Ribs calmly sitting in a nearby wood, took the cat back to his owner and calmly accepted the £200 reward.

*   *   *

A young couple in Oxford both arrived late at work with the least likely excuse ever concocted. Their cat, they alleged, had turned the hands of their alarm clock back by two hours!

*   *   *

Gladys Morton spent her life savings and 8 years searching for her cat Phoo. The 80-year-old spent hundreds of pounds on taxi fares and advertisements, trying to track down her missing Siamese seal-point. Even as the years went by, Mrs Morton refused to stop searching. Every day, she faithfully walked round the country lanes in St Ives, Cornwall, looking for her recalcitrant mog.

*   *   *

Mr and Mrs Paul Tabori of Hexham in Northumberland tried wooing their missing cat Melanie back home. They spent an entire day in a field boiling up pounds of cod – her favourite dish. Unfortunately, Melanie had bigger fish to fry (so to speak) and the Taboris went home unsuccessful. Instead, they tried the more conventional method of offering a £10 reward.

* * *

Blackie the cat was left £50,000 by his late owner. This paid for his dish of Whiskas twice a day and the occasional treat of salmon or white fish. After his inheritance, Blackie was especially lucky in having a choice of residence: he could choose between a kennel in the cattery or a cat basket in the house.

* * *

In the 1970s, two spinster friends paid to have their friends flown over from Kenya. The friends, 29 cats, cost £339 in quarantine fees alone. Whilst the cats were in quarantine, the women rented a flat nearby for 18 weeks and spent extra money on food and blankets for the animals. It also transpired that the cat-mad duo had paid for another deceased moggie to be flown from Kenya for burial in British soil.

* * *

Actress Beryl Reid, proud owner of 10 cats, tells of the time when she wanted to spend a penny and, heading for the loo, was narrowly beaten to it by one of her cats, Dimly. Living up to his name, Dimly missed the seat and knocked himself out on the toilet bowl, and Beryl had to perform artificial respiration to bring him round again! On another occasion, Dimly proudly presented Beryl with a moorhen which he had dragged in through the cat-flap and thoughtfully deposited in her bath. He later brought in a large rabbit which he left in the bureau. This time, Beryl, in her night-dress, had to carry the poor creature 20 yards down the lane, where she released him.

*   *   *

If your home is not big enough to swing a cat in, then buy a cat's cradle. This fur-fabric ham-mock which hangs from a radiator is specially designed to rock Tiddles to sleep in the warmest possible place. It was invented by a computer graphics designer for his arthritic Siamese, and is apparently a great hit with hep cats everywhere.

*   *   *

In 1986, Wilberforce the official Downing Street cat was retired. Wilberforce, a black and white neutered tom, was forced to join the rest of the unemployed in classic post-industrial style. A spokesman for Number 10 said, 'He was hired to keep the mice down, and was so good at his job that he has not been replaced.'

* * *

That political pooch Millie, The First Dog of the White House, was finally replaced by The First Cat, when the Bushes moved out and the Clintons moved in. A measure of Bush's popularity – or at least of the Americans' love of pets – had been Millie's spaniel autobiography, ghost-written by Barbara Bush and greatly outselling the President's own memoirs! Millie wasn't the first First Dog – the Reagans and the Lyndon Johnsons had blazed the trail – but America reacted with delight when Chelsea Clinton and 'Socks' took office. As might be expected, an animal behaviourist was quick to jump in with his theory of what effect Socks would have on the White House. He believed that the Clinton's cat was a symbol of a more gentle, introverted presidency. He mused, 'Cat owners tend to be private and sensitive people; dog owners are more outgoing and gregarious.'

Socksmania hit the USA almost before President Clinton had rolled his sleeves up in the Oval Office. *Time* magazine reported an immediate merchandizing blitz all over the country of Socks memorabilia in the form of books, soft toys, buttons, earrings, Move Over Millie T-shirts and note cards. Even smart New York store Bloomingdale's was selling a gold and enamel Socks tie-pin for $45.

*   *   *

In 1992, John Mann from Dumfriesshire set off in the car with his daughter Charlotte to do some shopping, completely unaware that her pet cat Honey Puss was sitting on the car roof. A neighbour saw them speed off with the cat clinging on for dear life, but was unable to stop them. After 3 miles, young Charlotte screamed that she had just seen Honey Puss fall off the roof of the car. Not surprisingly, John didn't believe her. Yet when they returned home, the ginger and white cat was nowhere to be seen. John admitted that Honey Puss' disappearance had devastated his daughter. 'When Charlotte said that Honey Puss had jumped off, I thought it was her imagination at work. He's been away for 3 days now and we're desperate to find him. Charlotte hasn't stopped crying.'

* * *

Some magpies were hoist by their own petard when Twitcher the cat decided she wanted to move into their nest. Having chased the birds away, Twitcher, blissfully unaware of whether it was 3 for a boy or 4 for a girl, settled down to give birth to 4 kittens. It didn't seem to matter that she was 30 feet up a tree ...

* * *

In 1992, scientists discovered that cats don't, as was thought, see in black and white but in shades of purple. Professor Rolf Paoli claimed that this extraordinary discovery would lead to a complete change in the way that cat food was packaged.

* * *

Evelyn Reeve's cat made sparks fly when it took refuge from a dog up a 50-foot pole.

Electrical workers had to cut the power to 800 homes in the area whilst the cat was rescued.

*   *   *

When 14-year-old Joe Bell heard the cries of pet kitten Rosie coming from somewhere in the kitchen, he called the fire brigade. The Bell family were convinced that Rosie had somehow got underneath the concrete kitchen floor, and told the firemen as much. The men tried in vain to get under the floor, but the kitten's agitated cries could still be heard. Next, the firemen tried knocking a hole in the wall; once again, they found nothing. After 3 hours of slowly reducing the kitchen to rubble, it was decided that Rosie was behind the blocked-off chimney. Sure enough, a hole was knocked into the chimney, and there was Rosie, covered in plaster. The kitten immediately tucked into some food, whilst the family were left surveying the damage. It is believed that Rosie fell down the chimney whilst climbing on the roof. John Bell, 16, explained, 'Rosie's very agile. She went out on Monday night, so God knows how long she was down there!'

*   *   *

Two days after a couple had moved into their new house in Wiltshire, firemen had to knock a hole in the wall to rescue their cat.

*   *   *

Bert, a plump black south London cat, went missing one Sunday morning from the house in Tooting he shared with Bob and Clare Collier. Nothing was heard from Bert until the following Wednesday, when Norman, the Colliers' other cat, was out in the garden and started an animated miaowed conversation with the missing mog. Still no one could trace where Bert's mews were coming from. Then the mystery was solved. Bert liked to hang out under the floorboards of the house next door, getting in through the hole left by an airbrick that had been absent for years. The Sunday that Bert disappeared, Bob and Clare's neighbour had finally got round to replacing the airbrick. Three days later, in order to liberate Bert, he had to take it out again.

*   *   *

Peaches the cat took refuge from the storm by slipping in between 2 houses, but it was only when she tried to leave that Peaches realized she was well and truly stuck. The RSPCA and firemen were called in to solve Peaches' predicament. It took them 9 hours to get her out of the 3½-inch gap, and cost £700. Finally, after all else failed, a house owner agreed to have part of his wall knocked down so that the cat could get out.

*   *   *

Mogadon the kitten fell 200 feet from the 21st floor of a Leeds tower block – and survived. The sleepy mog, who lived in a flat, had been inspecting the view from the open window when she found herself sailing through space. She landed in a bush, but after a trip to the vet was pronounced to be A1. It was calculated that she accelerated to a peak speed of of 112 feet per second, making her leap for glory last a total of 3.5 seconds.

*   *   *

Top Cat, a Devon tom, decided to try some French cuisine. But, obviously not a true gourmet, he ate a snail – complete with shell! Top Cat had to be rushed to the vet for emergency surgery to remove the offending gastropod.

*   *   *

Eric the cat was rather partial to a pub crawl, thus creating problems for his owner, Linda Drew from Devon. The ginger tom would cadge saucers of Guinness from drinkers in the local pub. Such was the generosity of the regulars that Eric would often be too drunk to find his way home and Linda would have to travel the 3 miles to the local to pick him up. Finally, Linda decided that Eric would become a teetotaller and kept him in with a customary saucer of milk until he learned how to handle his alcohol . . .

*   *   *

Cool cats after kicks took to sucking on kiwi fruit vines. The cats in Wellington, New Zealand had discovered (albeit unwittingly) that there was a chemical in the fruit which was similar to that found in catnip. It made them hallucinate.

*   *   *

Britta Zupfer, 27, returned from holiday to find her flat in Swansea, South Wales looking like a bomb had hit it. The furniture had been ripped to shreds and many ornaments had been broken. At first, Britta thought she'd been burgled, but nothing was missing. The next day, when some bread and chicken were stolen from the kitchen, she assumed she had rodents and called in the rat catchers. But after a thorough search the council pest control representative found the real root of the problem. He opened up Britta's piano and a white cat shot out, hissing and spitting, before disappearing out of the door. Britta said philosophically, 'It's no wonder the piano kept going out of tune.'

*　　*　　*

A quiet snooze in the washing machine for Shelley, a pedigree Persian, turned into a turbo-boost ride. Owner Daphne Baker, unaware that Shelley was peacefully dreaming in amongst the dirty clothes, switched the machine on. The cat was treated to two wash cycles and three spins before Daphne spotted a creature gazing out from the little window. She rushed the cat to the vet, but apart from a spot of concussion Shelley was given a clean – extremely clean – bill of health.

Betty the cat also went through two cycles of the washing machine before she was spotted. The cat, a Christmas present to 3-year-old Jessie Dane, was seen miaowing and pressing her face against the glass. Firemen were called in to rescue Betty from the spin-dry cycle, because of a fault in the automatic safety lock. Jessie's father Cliff announced, 'Luckily, Jessie slept through it all.'

*   *   *

The Drury family in Derby cancelled their holiday to the Lakes so that Tilly their cat could have life-saving plastic surgery. Tilly, who had been hit by a car, needed several expensive operations to try and restore her face. The family decided that Tilly's wellbeing was worth more than their two weeks away.

*   *   *

In America in the late 80s, pet owners concerned for kitty's mental health could book her in at an animal psychic's. For £35 per hour, the psychic would trawl kitty's karma to find the cause of her neuroses.

*   *   *

In 1992, a jet was delayed for 5 hours at Sydney airport until a stowaway was removed. Staff spent the time trying to shoo away the kitten that had hidden in the undercarriage ...

*   *   *

After several weeks, clergyman Bill East had finally given up all hope of ever seeing his tabby cat again. Then one evening, Father East sat down at the organ in St Luke's Church, Sunderland. 'I hit the first note,' he explained later, 'and she came flying out just above my head.' Sadly, however, this fleeting glimpse of flying feline was the last he saw of the cat. So terrified was she that, this time, she disappeared for good.

*   *   *

A stray cat caused havoc for Nicola Harrison and Neil Davies when he decided to hide in their chimney for 3 days. Despite the couple removing part of the brickwork, the cat refused to budge. The only time that she moved more than an inch was when they went out. Then Sooty, as they called her, came out and paraded across the carpet, leaving sets of black paw prints everywhere. Finally, when the chimney breast was half-dismantled, Sooty was lured out with a tin of pilchards.

*   *   *

Driver Vinod Patel, worried by the strange noises coming from his car engine, found a kitten in the gear box! Vinod said, 'I thought there was something wrong with my new Rover. It's a miracle the poor thing wasn't killed.' The joy-riding cat was duly named Rover and taken to an animal welfare centre.

*   *   *

Musician Mike Leander became concerned that his 2 Burmese cats, Shugi and Jem, had never left his house in London. Realizing that the pair had lived very sheltered lives, Mike took his Camcorder to Regent's Park Zoo, where he videoed snakes, birds and rabbits and played the tape back to his cats, who seemed to enjoy it. In fact, they enjoyed it so much that Mike approached pet psychologist Peter Neville, and between them they worked out the ultimate cat movie. The result was an hour long tape called *Cool For Cats*, which Peter claimed would stimulate frustrated or plain apathetic felines. The tape featured scenes of cats grooming and licking each other, as well as pictures of pigeons, rabbits and fish. Peter claimed that the video would 'put mouth-watering excitement and the spice of romance into the lives of lonely cats'. He added, 'So many get stuck indoors, when they should be outside meeting members of the opposite sex.' The tape also included an ultrasonic soundtrack which was inaudible to humans, but guaranteed to get your moggie hot under the collar. Mike added, 'My cats were driving me crazy, shredding curtains. Then it dawned on me that they might be lonely. This video should stimulate them – it's definitely not PG certificate!'

*   *   *

When Mickey the cat departed this world, his owner decided to have him stuffed by a taxidermist in south-east London. She paid her £40 deposit and waited for her eternally preserved Mickey to be returned in all his glory. However, after a costly legal battle which dragged on for 3 years, the distraught owner was left with only Mickey's skin tacked to a board. The taxidermist (who has since disappeared) admitted that Mickey had been somewhat difficult to preserve because of his age. In fact, when he put the cat into the freezer, it had failed to freeze properly. Eventually, when it became clear to everyone concerned that stuffing Mickey was out of the question, the taxidermist offered the owner the cat's remains in a bucket. 'That was hardly the same,' declared the owner. Instead, she had to content herself with Mickey's fur, which she framed and gave pride of place on the wall. But even the skin was not really satisfactory. 'He has no head and his paws are missing – he could be any cat,' she wailed.

2
The Dog's Tale

A woman in Chertsey, Surrey phoned the police with the dramatic news that she was being burgled – by a Labrador dog. Police collared the thieving hound, Paddy, as he made off with a watering can, and discovered that he had also nicked toys, carpets, clothes, a pedal bin and a car exhaust. His owner, Emma Cox, had to promise to keep her kleptomaniac animal under control.

*   *   *

A burglar in Oxfordshire absent-mindedly left his Jack Russell terrier accomplice behind when he robbed one house. When the police arrived, the dog was all too keen to lead them home – the dog's owner was jailed for 15 months.

*   *   *

In 1991, happily married couple Stewart and Josephine McSkimming were forced to live in separate houses – because their dogs didn't get on. Skirmishes between Jo's Labrador-cross, Tanya, and Stewart's springer spaniel, Gale, made life hell. So much so that the couple resigned themselves to separation until the demise of one or other of the dogs. The problems between the duelling dogs had been in evidence from an early stage. Even pacifying them with dog biscuits failed to do the trick, and whenever the two hounds met there was a near bloodbath. Once when Jo and Stewart tried to intervene, they both required hospital attention for dog-inflicted wounds. For the couple, living apart meant driving a total of 400 miles a week to spend time with each other – whilst the dogs stayed locked in separate cars. Obviously a die-hard romantic, Stewart said ruefully, 'We would like to get together, if only to cut down on the petrol.' Whilst Jo said, 'When it comes down to it, neither of us will sacrifice our dogs for each other.' The separation lasted 3 years. In 1993, Tanya died and the McSkimmings finally moved in together. They were said not to be looking for a replacement dog.

*　　　*　　　*

A lady called Ermintrude Phillips wrote to the *Daily Mail* in 1970, to tell readers of the most amazing experience she had had with her dog. Ermintrude related how one evening, the two of them were watching *Julius Caesar* on the television, and at Mark Antony's crucial speech: 'Cry havoc and let slip the dogs of war,' the dog got up and wagged its tail. The dog, or so Ermintrude concluded, thought Mark Antony had said, 'Let's take the dogs for a walk.'

*　　　*　　　*

A bar offering snacks and drinks for dogs opened in Novo Ligure, Italy in 1992. Owners can leave their pets to shoot the breeze with the other guys while they go shopping.

*　　*　　*

What may have been the prototype shaggy dog story unfolded in Camden Town, London in 1989, when Rosie, a truly shaggy hound, ran into a lift on her own and the doors jammed. Her owner, Joan Fantham, called the fire brigade, but whilst the firemen struggled to rescue Rosie, joyriders stole their fire engine, crashing it into 3 cars and demolishing 2 walls. As the fire engine careered crazily across north London, it was joined by an ambulance which gave chase, thinking the driver might be ill. The joyriders ran off after their last crash. Rosie was fine. Joan was 'terribly embarrassed'.

* * *

For most people, their dog is their best friend, but Ray Hobley, 62, of West Bromwich, West Midlands is less certain. Ray was made homeless when his Jack Russell puppy Sam turned pyromaniac. One day in 1993, Sam rubbed some matches together, set fire to his blanket and burned down Ray's council flat.

Dog owner Peter Rogers, of Andover, Hampshire, had even less cause to believe the best friend theory. His Newfoundland playfully jumped on his shoulders whilst he was swimming – and drowned him. Tragically, the children to whom he shouted and waved as he went under thought Peter and the dog were playing.

*   *   *

Jasper, a terrier from Atherton, Lancashire, mistook a can of hairspray for a bone, settled down by a gas fire to bite into it, and blew the house up, causing £3,000-worth of damage. His owners and their children ended up in hospital. Jasper escaped with a singed coat – and a life-long ban from being left alone inside the house.

*   *   *

That was nothing compared to the havoc wreaked by a long-haired collie named, or misnamed in this case, Lucky. Lucky ran out into the street, making a pensioner jump into the road. The old lady was injured by a passing lorry and sued the dog's owner, Patricia Segall. Mrs Segall, who was not insured, was landed with a bill for £5,000 – plus £75,000 costs.

*   *   *

Marriage guidance counsellors in Bath listened as a woman going through a divorce told them how her 9-year-old son had turned into an alcoholic – or so she thought. She had left a wine box on the kitchen table, and after a few days, realized it was half empty – knowing she had only taken a couple of glasses from it. Feeling guilty that the stress of the divorce might be having such an effect on her child, she decided to mention it to him tactfully. He denied having touched it. The pair then watched, amazed, as their Labrador turned the tap on the winebox, helped herself to a drink, then turned it off – and went for a quiet sleep.

*   *   *

A Toronto woman was having terrible trouble getting her weight down. She spent a fortune on diets and exercise classes, but every time she got on the bathroom scales it was the same depressing story. In fact, her weight seemed to be going up. It was only after several weeks of this misery that she discovered Wolf, her St Bernard, was putting a paw on the scales each time she stepped on them. She had been a perfect weight all the time – but had lost half a stone and got much fitter, thanks to Wolf.

Prince the mongrel was not renowned for his brain. He lived in a second-floor flat in Coventry and wanted to go walkies so much that he dashed out of the door – except that it wasn't the door – it was a window. Prince fell 35 feet and broke a tailbone.

Another canine would-be aviator smashed through a car windscreen in Chichester. The small brown dog, who was being chased by an Alsatian, launched itself off a high wall into the path of pensioners Donald and Peggy Barbrook. The couple were injured, but the flying dog ran off.

An airborne Airedale in Essen, Germany killed a 79-year-old woman when it leaped from a third-floor window and landed on her head. It too scampered off unharmed, grateful for the relatively soft landing.

*   *   *

Sue Chambers, a dog lover from Shotley Bridge, County Durham, knitted herself a jumper from the coats of her two dead Alsatians.

*   *   *

A poodle called Tina loved it when the coalman came to her house in Rotherham, Yorkshire. She would skip around excitedly in the passageway – until the day coalman John Gibson accidentally dropped a hundred-weight sack of coal on top her. Her owner Brian Leadbetter, aged 62, looked dolefully at the flattened Tina and said, 'That looks like a goner. Bloody hell, I've just fed her.' The coalman ended up unexpectedly digging a hole in the back garden for Tina to be popped in. Brian was most worried, because his wife Elsie, who treasured the poodle, was out for the day. 'She'll not be best pleased,' he quavered, during the long wait for her return.

*   *   *

Police sniffer dogs on the scent of a burglar in Southampton were put off the trail by a passing milkfloat that doubled as a grocery delivery service. They forgot all about the burglar and surrounded the float, baying.

*   *   *

A Rottweiler guard dog called Tyson was stolen in a raid on Robert Davies' waste removal firm near Chester.

*   *   *

Peter, a Border collie, drove his neighbours mad in Borstal, Kent – with his out of tune piano playing. Peter was taught to play by his owners, Barbara and Phillip Sym. Eventually, a trainer called Chuck Kemsley was brought in, at a cost of £35 per hour, to show Peter how to play with both paws and keep a rhythm, but the 7-year-old dog still had trouble getting the notes in the right order. His speciality was the *Coronation Street* theme tune. Reacting to his neighbours' complaints, Phillip, 70, said, 'It's not too bad, now he's had lessons. You should have heard him before.' The *Sun* newspaper, reporting the story in June 1993, helpfully suggested some other tunes for Peter to perfect: 'Yelp, I need Somebody', 'Please Re-Leash Me', 'Good Golly, Miss Collie' and 'Walkies On The Wild Side' ...

*   *   *

A 55-minute drama video for dogs was released in 1992. Entitled *Beastenders*, the £9.99 film, with a soundtrack allegedly in ultrasonic dog language, told the story of Ben, a springer spaniel, who nods off whilst watching *Eastenders*.

He dreams of chasing a Frisbee with a Rottweiler, sniffing lampposts and meeting his match in Rambo, a ferocious cat. Makers Jenny Jones and Graham Carter sold 500 copies of their movie.

* * *

Yorkshire terrier Benjy was left £20,000 to keep him in the lap of luxury until his whiskers went grey. Unfortunately, within 10 days of becoming a monied mutt, Benjy bit one of his late owner's relatives and had to be put down.

* * *

Top Parisian fashion houses have those essential items to make sure your mongrel is positively *à la mode*: Chaumet offers to bejewel your dog's jowls; Louis Vuitton go one step further – they have bags which are specially adapted in which to carry your pooch!

* * *

The cost of removing doggy donations from the pavements of Paris is estimated to be £30 per 100 grams. It has not gone unnoted among the French that this is a shade over the price of some pretty good *foie gras*.

* * *

Smudge, a 2-year-old Jack Russell, caused a rumpus when he got stuck in a rabbit hole. His owner Joseph Shawler, a businessman from Tattingstone, Suffolk, supervised the 18 youngsters who dug away at the maze of rabbit warrens in the field behind the Shawlers' house. After 4 days, when it was obvious that this method was not working, Joe hired a mechanical excavator for £80, intending to dig Smudge out that way. He needn't have bothered. Another Jack Russell succeeded where man and machine had failed, and dug Smudge out in minutes.

* * *

When two poodles got married (yes, really) in Palm Springs, USA they naturally invited all their 4-legged friends to the ceremony. The bride looked radiant in a full-length ivory satin gown with trimmings of lace and pearls, the pearl theme being echoed in the crown that held her veil firmly in place. To do his betrothed justice, the groom had dressed up like the proverbial dog's dinner. Similarly, the guests had spared no expense, and the congregation – all poodles – displayed a veritable flair for fashion. One dog, Gigi Kimberley, sported a pink sequinned evening coat embellished with a white mink collar, and two male poodles, Beau and Michael, wore matching coats in pink and yellow. After the ceremony, all the guests were invited for a celebratory meal.

*   *   *

Just like humans, dogs can have their noses pushed out of joint when there's an addition to the family. Rie Kano, 32, from Tokyo is a vet who has studied psychosomatic disorders in pets. She discovered that when an owner's love is directed elsewhere, the dog tends to suffer. Kano cited the case of the 6-year-old Maltese who was the beloved pet of a couple in their 50s. The dog had received bags of attention until the couple acquired their first grandchild. Feeling left out, the dog started to take the baby's blanket and would bite his own feet until they bled. Similarly, a 6-year-old dachshund was so close to its owner that it would hop in the tub with her whenever she took a bath. When the owner had a baby and gave the dog less attention, the dog, although fully house-trained, started to pee on the floor.

*   *   *

Singer Whitney Houston spent £28,000 on a 10-foot-high replica of her New Jersey mansion for her Japanese Akita dogs, Lucy and Ethel. The superkennel, with soft lighting, central heating, running water and a loo, was never put to use, however. Whitney decided she would miss the hounds scampering around her own house.

*   *   *

Ex-military policeman Bill Raylor, 83, of Clacton-on-Sea, Essex celebrated the Gulf War by wrapping his Labradors, Honey and Cindy, in the flag. The dogs had to wear Union Jack coats for walkies until the war was over.

*   *   *

In Paignton, Devon, Geoff Robinson's mastiff

pup chewed up Geoff's 88-year-old great-aunt's dentures! Sentence: pup banned from chocolate treats until new teeth paid for.

* * *

In 1990, Jennifer Corker gave up her job and enrolled at the Royal College of Art to concentrate on dog jewellery. When asked why she had chosen such a career, she replied, 'Why-ever not? Animals are vain too.' Jennifer's own whippet, named Paris, bore testament to her theory. He sported a sterling silver collar with leather backing, decorated with dancing dogs, a crown and a squirrel. When Jennifer explained these symbols, it transpired that the silver dog was the vain Paris and the crown represented a royal park where he had killed his first squirrel. Jennifer also incorporated bells on to her dog's collar, so that any wild life in his vicinity had a bit of a chance. The collars cost between £600 and £1,700. Jennifer said she preferred to meet the dog in person, as it were, so that she could design jewels that would reflect its character.

* * *

Forty-five years after his death, Battle of Britain hero Wing Commander Guy Gibson ran into a bit of flak concerning the political correctness of his dog. The Royal Canadian Airforce Association ran a picture in its magazine of the Dam Busters ace with Canadian members of his squadron and his black Labrador. They did not reckon that captioning the photo with the dog's name would cause any problems. Well, OK, it was Nigger, but it needed the New Brunswick Human Rights Commission to take the matter with due seriousness, nearly half a century later. This august body put in an official complaint that the caption had 'blatant racist overtones' and was 'offensive and inappropriate'. The RCAA had to issue a statement spelling out the fact that nigger was the name of a colour in the 1930s and that the last thing Guy Gibson had been was racist.

* * *

The guests had gathered in an up-market New York restaurant to say goodbye to their esteemed friend. The host was Fellow, a 9-year-old schipperke who suffered from a dodgy ticker. Fellow's owner, Mrs Michele

Bertotti, had obviously decided that before anything terminal happened to her pet, it was only fitting that a farewell party should be held in his honour. The guests dined on liver pâté, steak tartare, beef stew and shrimp, with a lightly-baked iced cake for dessert. Their owners contented themselves with quaffing champagne, while the dogs wolfed down their meals as politely as possible. Fellow received some parting gifts from his friends in the shape of rubber toys and a box of malted milk tablets. Larry Apodaca, who had accompanied his 2 poodles to the bash, was rather moved by the whole affair. He remarked with evident emotion, 'Dogs are so loyal, faithful and honest. How often do you find that among humans any more?'

*　　　*　　　*

Police laid siege to a flat for 2 hours before discovering that the violent suspect they were after was, in fact, a dog. The officers saw a curtain twitch at the Birmingham flat where they believed an armed man was hiding out. The block was surrounded and special nego-tiators with megaphones repeatedly invited the occupant of the flat to come out and talk.

Finally, they broke in . . . to find a dozy Alsatian that had been left on its own.

*   *   *

Penny, a lost Jack Russell, slipped her lead in Williton, Somerset, then went of her own accord to wait patiently to be reclaimed – outside the police station.

*   *   *

A couple from Florida were so distraught when their little mongrel Sweetie died of a heart attack that they had her freeze-dried. This process – similar to what happens to instant coffee – took 3 months and cost owners 71-year-old Steve Kocsis and his wife Vivienne $575. Now, however, it means that Sweetie can still sleep, so to speak, in her own bed, covered by a quilt and surrounded by dog food and a bowl of filtered water. Each morning, the couple draw back Sweetie's cover, hold her and ask her how she slept, brushing aside the fact that she has been dead and freeze-dried for the last 2 years. Vivienne admitted, 'My sister thinks I'm looney.' She also revealed that she had had her canary freeze-dried when he had 'fallen from his perch'. She added, 'I'd do my husband too, but he doesn't want it.'

*   *   *

If guard dogs are altogether too much trouble, why not try a Super Doggy Guard One, produced by the Japanese firm Nomura Toys? Super Doggy is a mechanical replica of the real McCoy, and is filled with infra-red sensors that make it bark every time anything moves. Dog lovers with a preference for something a little less aggressive can opt for the little puppy implanted with a voice-recognition mechanism. It is guaranteed to yelp and wag its tail when you call out its name.

*   *   *

Dog psychologist Dr Roger Mugford warned divorcing couples not to forget the feelings of their hounds during a break-up. Dr Mugford, who sees an average 2,000 dogs a year at his clinics in Chertsey, Manchester and Paris, claims that dogs are extremely sensitive to tensions within a family. He further cautions that a major change like a split-up can make dogs become destructive. Not surprisingly, considering the royal family's marital problems, Dr Mugford's clients include the Queen, to whom he gave a special whistle to stop the Corgis fighting. He also advised President Bush on troubles he had with Millie, the famed White House mutt. Other celebrity clients have included Silky, a cross-bred Alsatian that started to have trouble when her owners, actors Dennis Waterman and Rula Lenska, were splitting up. 'Poor Silky has suffered bouts of aggression since the break-up, but tenderness cures,' the therapist said. Other celebrity dog owners confirm the Mugford theory. Katie Boyle recalls her dog Tessa becoming nasty when she got divorced 23 years ago, and Susan George watched her red setters snap and snarl at each other for the first time when her long relationship with singer Jack Jones was on the rocks. Jilly Cooper's mongrel Barbara also senses tension between her and husband Leo. 'If Leo is angry with me, she starts to whine at him, which makes us both laugh and stops us rowing,' Jilly says.

To prevent pets from turning into hounds from hell, Dr Dog suggests that owners play a tape recording of a busy day in the house to keep their pets happy whilst they are out.

*   *   *

In Belgium, dogs of divorcing couples are treated with the same respect as children. A mongrel there called Ben became caught up in a tug-of-hate case. The Belgian appeal court overturned a divorce ruling that gave Emile Desmet the right to take Ben for walks every Saturday, so long as the dog did not come in contact with his new girlfriend's dog. Mr Desmet's ex-wife Marianne won the right to keep Ben all to herself.

*   *   *

Paul Brunt was asked to pay part of the £400 it had cost to dig his terrier out of an underground drainpipe. This posed a problem, since Paul was unemployed. Luckily, the pet-loving public flooded the RSPCA with enough donations to pay the entire bill 2½ times over!

*   *   *

Police went to a house in Arkesden, Essex when a heavy breather called the operator. They found a dog had accidentally called 100 while chewing the phone lead.

*   *   *

Dick Crossman, a leading minister in Harold Wilson's cabinet, once visited the Queen. With the kind of tact that a few centuries earlier would have reserved him a room in the Tower, he informed Her Majesty that his poodle, Suki, could do a better job of rounding up cattle than any corgi. He also described the royal dogs as 'fat' and 'the colour of the carpet'.

*   *   *

In 1989, Pam Cunningham started making Burberries for dogs, and the sheepskin-lined waterproofs sold in their thousands. The coats were available in Harrods and Selfridges and as far away as Japan. Such a coat for a great Dane would set you back £29, but, Pam reasoned, 'People are happy to pay more for quality.'

*   *   *

When a mongrel called Trixie ran recklessly into the road, her owner May Moss ran recklessly after her. Unfortunately, she was struck by a moped and died. Not content, Trixie ran off for a second time, this time with May's husband James in hot pursuit. James also died – trying to protect the jinxed mutt from an express train.

*　　*　　*

Dog owner John Molloy discovered that the maxim 'one good turn deserves another' is equally upheld in the dog world. One day in the middle of winter John was out in a snow-storm, walking his 2 dogs by an iced-up river. When one dog took a flying leap on to the ice and disappeared through it, John didn't think twice. Jumping in after the hapless hound, he managed to throw it to the safety of the bank, but then couldn't pull himself out. Using his ingenuity, John untied the 2 leads from round his waist, joined them together and threw them to his Labrador on the bank. Bracing her back legs and getting a good grip on the leads with her teeth, the dog managed to pull her master – all 11½ stone of him – out on to the safety of the bank.

*　　*　　*

An Airedale called Rolf was attributed with the

powers of ESP. Rolf was a genius at sums, could count up to 100 and knew the alphabet. Once, when he was asked the meaning of the word 'autumn', Rolf spelt out his reply with a paw: 'the time for apples'.

*   *   *

Joseph Wylder, author of the seminal book *Psychic Pets*, also suggested that animals need to be kept informed about what their owners are up to around the house. He believed that explaining tasks such as cooking and cleaning to your pooch could help you to develop a more mutual understanding. Furthermore, he added, when your dog gazes at you with those puppy eyes, don't automatically assume he wants walkies or din-dins. Sometimes, claimed the pet expert, he really wants you to play him some classical music or to read him a story.

*   *   *

In the 1950s, a beagle appeared on American TV under the title of Chris the Mathematical Mongrel. Chris could subtract, multiply and divide numbers by tapping the answers on the questioner's arm.

*   *   *

Ronald and Betty Metherall of Kings Langley in Hertfordshire were so upset when their 11-year-old dog Lassie went missing that they offered the ultimate reward to anyone who could help get her back – the roof over their heads. Betty said, 'If anyone had demanded our £30,000 house in return for Lassie, we would have moved into a caravan rather than lose her.' luckily for them, Lassie was found in a nearby wood by a local farmer – who refused to take any reward.

*   *   *

One Mr Austin of Stockport, Cheshire offered £200 plus his ancient but serviceable car to anyone who could find his missing dog. The bull-terrier, named Caesar, was found by a man who already had a car, so he was given an extra £100 instead.

*   *   *

Charles Day took to the skies trying to find his missing Labrador. Charles, an estate agent from Nottingham, hired a helicopter for £50 an hour and spent 4 hours looking down on fields for his wayward hound. Eventually, Chris spotted his dog just 3 miles from his house, but insisted, 'it was worth every penny'. Exactly the thoughts of Tim and Angela Charlesworth of Orston, Nottinghamshire. When their Russian wolf-hound Scarlett went missing and radio appeals for her return came to nothing, they too hired a helicopter and pilot to search for their dog, at a cost of £460. They found her in a field 4 miles from home and airlifted her to safety.

*　　*　　*

Sir John Cowperthwaite, former Financial Secretary to the Hong Kong government, flew all the way from Hong Kong to London to search for his wife's pet, after Bluey the Alsatian had happily chewed his way out of quarantine kennels at Heathrow Airport. The total cost for the trip came to over £800, but at least it was successful. Sir John finally found the unrepentant hound in Hayes, Middlesex.

Timmy the terrier also gnawed his way out of quarantine in Australia. Owners Mr and Mrs Gordon Marshall travelled 2,000 miles from their home town of Mount Isa in hot pursuit, and eventually found him in Sydney.

*　　*　　*

A new trend was started by teenage girls in Paris. Instead of going baby-sitting, they chose to dog-sit instead. Their reasoning was financial. Why look after *le petit* Phillipe for £4 an hour when you could supervise Fido for the astonishing going rate of £8?

*　　*　　*

A dog dating agency in Santa Monica, California asked in an advertisement: 'Is your hound lonely or inhibited?' If the answer was in the affirmative, the agency promised to put owners of lovesick or wallflower doggies in touch with one another.

*　　*　　*

In the early part of the 70s, Americans could buy all manner of accessories for the dog who had everything: car safety-belts for the dog who liked to travel, bikinis for the beach, ski-suits for the suave, TV lounging robes for the relaxed, sequinned cocktail coats for the pretentious, plastic Batman coats for dare-devil dogs and rollerskates for the cool. Dogs with time on their paws could get stuck into a squeaking slipper, an (artificial) cat that yelled when bitten or a chocolate-flavoured monkey head. Beds for dogs became best-sellers, ranging from the electrically heated foam-cushion cabana, to the fibre-glass igloo. Dogs with an interest in the Wild West could even buy the Prince Valiant suede tent. Canine couture aside, pets could also be treated to health insurance, gourmet foods, jewellery and, of course, their own coats of arms. To cash in on the emotions involved in motherhood, came the *Puppy's Baby Book*. Available in either pink or blue, there were pages for paw prints, growth measurements, illnesses, birthdays and Christmas presents. There was even a special page to commemorate the date of puppy's first bark . . .

Mildred Pell's 'Canine Creations' in Manhattan offered made-to-measure clothes for the dog in your life. From white dinner jackets to silver lamé cocktail capes, your pooch could be dressed like a dog's dinner. All clothes required fittings.

*   *   *

At the 1974 British Pet Trade fair in Harrogate,

Yorkshire an Edinburgh firm came up with the ultimate beauty products for poodles. They marketed 12 different colours of nail vanish and tear sticks, which removed discolouration from around the eye area. Presumably, they were designed for when one's pooch's mascara smudged . . .

* * *

A Milan opera lover, who hated leaving her dog at home whilst she went to concerts, aimed to get the best of both worlds by taking her dog to an animal trainer. The trainer taught the pooch not to bark and also to curl himself round the woman's shoulders so that he looked, to all intents and purposes, just like a fur collar. In this manner, the woman sneaked her pet unnoticed into the opera on many occasions.

* * *

Beauty, a toy poodle, had the best in life. She had her own room complete with furniture and decorations, and her own closet complete with pyjamas, dressing gown, slippers and three fur coats. Beauty also had the love of her doting American owner. Such was the bond between poodle and owner that when the woman went on holiday for a few days without her, Beauty had a nervous breakdown and had to be taken for psychiatric help.

*   *   *

In 1966 a court heard how Mrs Maureen Ann Lewis had a husband who was personable, well-off, immaculate and ambitious. Maureen, however, sought a divorce from him on the grounds of cruelty to their Border collie, Laddie. Instead, when the divorce judge heard the whole story, he granted Mr Lewis a decree nisi because of his wife's cruelty. The court heard how Laddie was Maureen's whole life. The dog not only slept in the matrimonial bedroom, but also in the matrimonial bed. The couple finally split up after an incident in which Mr Lewis moved a chair to make way for a visitor in front of the TV set. Somehow he stepped on or bumped into the dog, who yelped. Mrs Lewis, incensed because her husband didn't apologize to Laddie, punched him. She then refused to cook for him. After going without tea that day, breakfast and lunch the next day, Mr Lewis left.

*   *   *

In 1963, a firm in Chicago came up with perfume for dogs. The concoctions for canines were Le Chien No 5, a 'light scent for those summer days' and Arf-Peggio, a 'stronger, spicier smell'. These pongy preparations cost just under £1 a bottle. Not to be outdone, other exhibitors at the American Pet Products Manufacturers Association offered over a dozen different deodorants for pets. One exhibitor explained earnestly that more feminine scents were used for cats, whilst the products for dogs were more like aftershave lotions.

*　　*　　*

American president Lyndon Johnson started a public outcry when he picked up one of his dogs by the ears during a photo session. Naturally the dog yelped and the people, naturally, complained. The *New York Daily News* even went as far as to admonish the President, declaring 'there is no excuse that we know of for anybody doing that. When a President does, it sets a bad example to any number of thoughtless children and callous adults ... and conceivably it loses the dog-earlifting President several million animal-lovers' votes.'

The President obviously took great heed of this criticism. The next time he was photographed with his beagles, he took care to hold them by their chests. Then, addressing the dogs, he added, 'Don't yelp now or you'll be quoted.'

*   *   *

An English baronet, who left his Pekinese behind when he went on a business trip to America, took to calling the dog up to 3 times a day. When the peke heard his master's voice coming all the way from across the Atlantic, he recognized it and licked the telephone. And, as he didn't pine, the baronet said that the £100-plus phone bill was well worth it.

*   *   *

A policeman served extra time in the force because of his dog. The bobby stayed on for 5 years longer than he needed, because he could not bear to be parted from his police dog. Both man and beast finally retired together.

*   *   *

Timmy the dog (no relation to the Famous Five) was kindly left £1,000 by his owner, ensuring that the cost of his keep would be covered for several years to come. Timmy's expenses came to £2 a week for his daily rations of half a can of beef *cat* food and some dog biscuits. The legacy also meant that Timmy could never be evicted from his palatial 6-foot by 4-foot carpet-lined kennel.

*   *   *

Perhaps the biggest dog rescue operation ever, involved Sam the Jack Russell, who became trapped in a quarry in Gwent. Sam was retrieved after a fortnight during which 100 tons of rocks were removed from the side of the quarry. Another giant rescue operation was mounted in April 1993, when Rastus, a 5-year-old black and tan Border terrier belonging to Peter and Pam Drake of Keighley, West Yorkshire disappeared down a hole in pursuit of a rabbit. For a week, RSPCA workers, police, firemen and volunteers dug with spades and bare hands in atrocious weather. In the end, a crane was used to remove heavy boulders, while the team of 20 tried to trace where Rastus' whimpering was coming from.

Eventually, a fibre-optic camera caught sight of his shape 25 feet underground, and Les Rushworth, 23, crawled into a hole to pull out the bedraggled, hungry mutt. The high-tech operation cost the RSPCA hundreds of pounds.

*　　*　　*

Philip Ray, in his book *Animal Antics*, recounts the story of Bruce, a guard dog who forgot to do his duty and ended up suffering from a guilt complex. Bruce tamely allowed burglars to shut him quietly in a bedroom whilst they got away with an £8,000 haul. As a result of the break-in, which took place at his owner's Georgian mansion in Yorkshire, Bruce suddenly developed eczema. His vet thought the skin disorder was caused by feelings of remorse because he had failed his owners. A British Veterinary Society spokesman added, 'He may have felt a sense of failure. He could have been thinking, "I'm ashamed. I'm a disaster."'

Philip Ray also recalled the case of a jury in a 8-week trial trooping off together so that one of the 12 good 'men' and true could feed his Alsatian. The juror was concerned that his 3-year-old pet would become disorientated whilst the case continued, so the entire jury was treated to a mystery detour which allowed the owner to be dropped off to feed his dog and take him for walk. Both man and beast were accompanied by a court usher, whilst the rest of the jury remained aboard the bus in the presence of another usher. Court officials could not recall any other occasion when 12 people were sent off to feed a dog, but they did remember a policeman being despatched once to feed a female juror's goldfish.

*   *   *

In a 1993 special issue of *Time* magazine devoted to animal intelligence, Michael D. Lemonick, an associate editor, told of golden retriever Newton who, he was convinced, had a perverse sense of humour. 'Whenever I tossed out a Frisbee for him,' Lemonick wrote, 'he'd take off in hot pursuit but then seem to lose track of it. Trotting back and forth only a yard or two from the toy, Newton would look all around, even up into the trees. He seemed genuinely baffled. Finally, I'd give up and head into the field to help him out. But no sooner would I get within 10 feet of him than he would invariably dash straight over to the Frisbee, grab it and start running like mad, looking over his shoulder with what looked suspiciously like a grin.'

3
All Creatures

Pigeon fancier Pat Lees of Sheffield had been waiting 40 years to win the prestigious France to England race. Then, in 1992, his greatest ever bird Percy put in an Olympic performance, flapping furiously all the 536 miles from Royan, south-west France, to Yorkshire, beating 1,000 other pigeons. The £150 first prize was in the bag as Percy flopped down exhausted outside his loft. Then a ginger tom called Sylvester leapt out from a bush and ate him. All Pat was left with was the indigestible bits, an identity tag – and a sympathetic posthumous third place. Distraught, Pat, who had lost 11 other birds to Sylvester that year, kept his £500-pigeon's remains in the fridge for a day as a mark of respect before dumping his champion in the dustbin.

*　　*　　*

When Mrs Ruth Durbin of Nailsea, near Bristol saw a budgerigar perched on her garden fence, she assumed it was lost. Imagine her surprise when, in a recognizably local accent, the bird chirped, 'My name is Pip. I live at number 7 Strawberry Close, Nailsea,' adding gruffly, 'Have you got that?' and hopping on to Mrs Durbin's hand. When she took it to its home, where owner Mr Arthur Bendon, 72, had given up hope of finding the bird and replaced it with a new one, she realized the bird's voice was identical to Mr Bendon's. 'I spent months teaching him to say his name and address, in case something like this happened,' Mr Bendon commented. He gave the £9 replacement bird to Mrs Durbin as a reward for returning Pip. With a 50-word vocabulary, Pip was clearly very talented, but the record for a talking bird remains with an African Grey parrot belonging to Iris Frost of Seaford, Sussex. This bird can say 800 words.

*　　*　　*

A goat in Kenya was put in jail for 2 days after being accused of stealing approximately 50p. The thieving creature had dipped its head into a lady fruit-seller's bag, and run away with the money. By the time the goat had been captured and taken to the police in Kilgoris, west of Nairobi, the animal had done what any experienced thief would do in the circumstances – eaten the evidence. Nevertheless, the goat was held in the cells until its owner repaid the money.

*   *   *

All things considered, it was probably just not Ingrid Hannoway's day. First, she turned up at Birmingham airport to board a flight home to Belfast with her pet tarantula, Boris, then security staff suggested that it might be safer if Boris were to travel in the hold. Ingrid, a caring tarantula owner, didn't think that would be very nice for her arachnid friend, so she posted him home in an envelope. Postmen freed Boris and told the RSPCA, who successfully brought a prosecution for cruelty.

*   *   *

The day of his big show in a hotel in Newquay was not George Williams' finest hour. Everything was going fine until George, a snake charmer who had picked up his craft in India, was bitten by his 6-foot Indian cobra. The 250-strong audience, thinking this was part of the show, roared their appreciation. They were not even alarmed when the snake slithered towards their tables. They did begin to smell a rat, however, when George stuffed the snake into its basket, slashed his hand with a knife and started sucking for dear life. An ambulance rushed him to hospital whilst a police car picked up serum from Paignton Zoo. In hospital, when asked why the snake had not been defanged, George said he thought it was cruel. Back at the hotel, meanwhile, manager Stan Pickles proudly announced that the show would go on.

*　　　*　　　*

Mrs Diane Cobb of Royston, Hertfordshire paid £49 for a tortoise which she took home and called Basil. Basil soon showed every sign of being very poor value as tortoises go. For days he remained static, refusing to poke his head outside his shell even for tempting vegetables like celery, cucumber and lettuce. It then occurred to Mrs Cobb that her initial suspicion, that Basil was dead, was correct, and she phoned Mr Timothy Reason, who had advertized the reptiles in *Exchange and Mart*. Mr Reason suggested that Basil was shy. Mrs Cobb, against her better judgement, gave the tortoise another week before taking him back to Mr Reason. 'He held it in his hand close to his head and shook it, as if trying to put some life back into him,' Mrs Cobb recounted at Luton Magistrates' Court, where Mr Reason stood accused of keeping a pet shop without a licence. Basil had, indeed, been dead all along – but Mr Reason was found not guilty of the charge.

*   *   *

Loopy Colonel Gaddafi of Libya likes to take a bit of home with him when he travels abroad. This means he attends conferences, wherever they might be held, with a Bedouin tent – and a complete caravan of camels. But according to the Roman historian Suetonius, the emperor Caligula was just a bit more bonkers: he nominated his horse as a new consul. The horse lived in a richly decorated marble stable with an ivory manger, had its own slaves, and stood at the head of table at dinner parties.

*   *   *

Susan Evans of Hove, Sussex banned her builder husband Mick from sleeping with her after he insisted on bringing a goose called Gazza to bed. Gazza would peck at Susan and even try to stop her getting into bed. Finally, Susan got her way and Gazza was thrown out at night ... but not before Mick had, with the ultimate in chivalry, said, 'Gazza was more cuddly than the wife in bed, and he didn't snore like her.'

*   *   *

In 1989, a gentleman called Jim Chapman from San Diego, California had a heart attack which left him clinically dead for 4 minutes. When Jim came round he was surprised – although not as surprised as his friends – to discover he had developed an obsession with llamas. This new and inexplicable fixation soon impelled him to replant his garden to resemble a corner of Peru. Jim then introduced 10 llamas into the garden, which he said was an act of thanks to

God for his recovery. Jim grew so fond of his
herd that he encouraged them to watch television with him.

*   *   *

According to that great chronicler of the quirky,
Lucinda Lambton, a gentleman named Mr
Cooke once came to believe that he was a fox.
To prove his point he spent 20 years under-
ground.

*   *   *

Firemen rescuing a horse from quicksand at
Ryde, on the Isle of Wight, failed to notice that
while they were busy hauling it up, their
£12,000 Land-rover was sinking at equal
speed. The vehicle was never seen again.

*   *   *

During 1990, the Americans developed a
passion for Vietnamese pot-bellied pigs. In
Asia, these pigs are more often found as dish of
the day than as a pet, but in the USA they
became *the* stylish present to give to your
loved one. Their selling point was that,

although they were pig-ugly, they were affectionate and didn't leave hair all over the place.
But relationships between pigs and owners
had to be good, since the pigs could live for up
to 35 years and grow to 130 pounds. However,
they were receptive to training. One breeder
proudly claimed: 'I taught him to sit up and
beg in 20 minutes.' Other owners tried to teach
their pigs to walk on hind legs, and one
optimist even tried to share his hobby with his
pig – skateboarding. On Los Angeles
boulevards, pot-bellied pigs were whizzed
round town in the passenger seat of sports
cars. Yet not everyone greeted these gi-
normous grunters with enthusiasm. The
science advisor at ASPCA in New York
demystified the glamour of the exotic pets by
announcing unsportingly: 'They're swine.'

One morning, in the rush-hour traffic on New
York's 42nd Street, a cabbie who had stopped
at lights shouted over to a man sitting in an
open top sports car. 'Say,' he yelled, 'is that a
pig sitting in your front seat?' Sure enough, a
black snout popped up out of the window.
'Sure,' said the other man proudly, 'but he's
not any pig. He's Francis as in Sir Francis
Bacon.'

Kayla Mull, 38, was one of the first pig-sellers

to operate in her hometown of Norco in California. Her pet, called Pignacious, won her over by being naturally neat, without smell or fleas. He would climb into bed with her and her husband Tom. When asked what it was like sharing his sleeping quarters with a 75-pound hog, Tom replied, 'A bit like sleeping with a hairbrush.'

New York pig-owners Ronald and Mary Kalish loved every aspect of their pet, Frank. Mary recalls how Frank preferred to watch cartoons and Westerns, and if the channel was switched he would protest by howling. In New York, there is a telephone hot-line for owners with pig problems, a pig training book and an advertising agency which suggests that you 'Go the whole hog. This is the time of the swine.'

*　　*　　*

The Monk family in Balham, south London were the proud owners of a pot-bellied pig named Lo Hung Tum – a name that is funnier when said than read. Despite being an impressive 7 stone, the Monks happily took Lo Hung Tum on holiday twice before finding out that they were not supposed to move her round the country without a licence. Mrs Monk said, 'She was a wonderful pet, very easy. But the RSPCA is right – they are a responsibility and once a month when they are on heat they get a bit stroppy.' Unfortunately, Lo Hung Tum could not resist snacking on some tasty, but highly poisonous laburnum leaves and promptly died. The Ministry of Agriculture warned owners of pot-bellied pigs that they could face fines of up to £2,000 if they broke regulations surrounding such pets. Owners would have to apply for a certificate which would allow them to take the pigs for walks on a lead and they had to stick to approved routes when exercising their swine. In extreme cases, the penalty for disregarding the regulations could be the demise of the pig.

*   *   *

A buyer for Harrods, meanwhile, was reputed to have kept his 4-foot pot-bellied pig at home – he lived in a flat. And Caren McLoughlin of Bromley, Kent dumped her boyfriend in favour of a pet pig called Kosher, who liked to snuggle up in bed between the couple. 'There was no competition,' she said. 'Kosher stayed.'

*   *   *

Kay and Geoff Stewart were so delighted with the manners and demeanour of their pot-bellied pig Colin, that they bought another called Hilary. This, unfortunately, was a bad move, for Colin was not best pleased with the competition. He turned from a fun-loving pig who liked a romp in the garden into a sulky swine who moped indoors. The Stuarts watched aghast as their darling piglet turned into a hellish hog. They told of the time they had refused him entry into the new kitchen cupboards to look for food ... so in retaliation he tore a strip off the new lino with his teeth. Furthermore, Colin was utterly mean to Hilary. She would follow him around with adoration in her little piggy eyes, whilst he would either ignore her completely or knock her out of the way. The only exception to this appeared to be when Hilary was on heat. Geoff explained, 'He won't leave her alone. For I week out of every 4 they're constantly bonking. That's a bit embarrassing when people come round.' Kay added that the swine had been in full swing when 'My mother saw them at it in the hall and left. She says she'll never stay here again.'

*　　　*　　　*

The pig-mania of the early 90s turned sour when owners discovered that the cute snouty pets eventually turned into big fat porkers. The fickle owners then started their own craze of 'pig dumping'. Animal rescuers found these pigs, which cost about £5,000 each, tied to trees in parks or abandoned in the country-side. Experts claimed that owners were neither prepared for their pigs to reach 130 pounds, nor for the difficulties of house-training them.

*   *   *

In 1992 in Japan, it was reported that every evening a badger would amble into a karaoke coffee shop to listen to the music. The badger turned up promptly at 8 p.m. in the shop in Yamato-Koriyama city, just in time to hear a local female professional singer. As an added attraction, the owner of the shop placed breadcrumbs and fried fish in the garden for the badger to nibble during the performance. Locals believed that the badger was a music lover and came solely to enjoy the singing. One said, 'He likes the karaoke music' whilst his friend remarked that the badger had even gone to the extent of 'learning the song'. A local zoologist unsportingly put the kibosh on their explanation by concluding that the badger had come to associate the singing of songs with there being food to eat.

*   *   *

Kae Khae Saepham of California became so furious with his wife that he beat her around the head with a frozen dead squirrel. The incident, which occurred after a heated argument between the couple, led to Mr Saepham being kept in custody under suspicion of wife beating. However, nothing was said about cruelty to animals. Police admitted that they had no idea what prompted Mr Saepham to keep frozen squirrels in his freezer in the first place.

*   *   *

Mega-star vet James Herriot, when asked what was the funniest animal-related thing that ever happened to him, related this story: 'When I'd been training about 3 days at veterinary college in Glasgow, they'd been showing us pictures of animals. There was a big picture on the wall of a horse, pointing out where you could get things like bog spavin, and I was thinking, I wish I could look at a real horse. But anyway, I still thought, well, I've learned something today. So I walked down later to Charing Cross in Glasgow, and I saw a coal horse. And I thought, now here we are, all these people are passing this coal horse and nobody knows what I know about horses. So I went up and gave him a friendly pat on the head to establish rapport. Immediately, he bent down and grabbed me by the shoulder, (and me in my nice new riding mac which I'd bought especially to join the college) and lifted me up into the air with his big teeth. I was just hanging there in the middle of a busy street. A great crowd gathered round me and there was a lot of pulling at me, but that horse just wouldn't let go. People were starting to laugh at me, then finally the coalman came down from the tenement and yelled at the horse to drop me, and he did, straight into the gutter. Then the coalman just said to me, "Dinnae meddle with things you know nothing aboot."'

A few years later, when he was qualified, Herriot found himself working with a Yorkshire vet who, for some reason he never discovered, did not like him. The patient was a cow giving birth, and the vet asked Herriot, who was temporarily his assistant, to put on a huge yellow rubber suit which did up right up to the neck. 'There I was,' he recalled, 'this apparition in rubber. The farmer obviously knew the vet, but didn't know me, and realized I was clearly going to do something terrific if I needed that outfit. They watched me and watched me as the old vet removed the afterbirth. The vet had given me a pessary to hold, and he said, "Right, hand me the pessary." I was a man in a suit of armour, and that was all I had to do.'

* * *

Organizers of an annual worm-charming competition in Devon had to introduce new rules to stop an outbreak of cheating which led to 3 teams being banned for life. Water, wine, lager and even clog dancing are acceptable ways of coaxing worms to the surface at the competition, held in Blackawton, but cheats had started adding washing-up liquid and other irritants to the water to chivvy the worms along. Now contestants have to drink the water to prove it is pure.

* * *

In 1990, an Italian craze for designer pets got out of hand when a black panther, whose owner never came forward, roamed the streets of Rome for 5 months. The panther was named 'Bagheera' (after Kipling's *Jungle Book* panther) by Italian newspapers, and caused uproar amongst the public and local farmers. Rumours accrediting the death of 30 sheep in a single night to this black panther caused some farmers to take their own action. Ivo Senzacqua was one such, who claimed he had seen the panther kill a calf. So Ivo sat in a tree all night, armed with a shotgun in case Bagheera returned. Realizing that some people thought his story was the product of an over-imaginative mind, Ivo said hotly, 'They're calling me a mad man, a fantasist. But ask anyone round here. I'm not a teller of tales – I saw it with my own eyes.' Other people suffered too. Residents refused to allow their children to play outside until the panther was caught, whilst one housewife, Maria Jacoponi, complained that the beast was stopping her children from going jogging. Meanwhile, lion tamers were conscripted to catch the animal. On several occasions, police and forest rangers were called out to scenes of reported sightings, only to return empty-handed. Police switchboards were constantly jammed with details of sightings, but most of these turned out to be domestic cats and dogs. Yet every cloud has a silver lining, for police following up one lead, once again failing to track down the elusive panther, stumbled across another exotic pet, a bear called Jimmy, who had given his owner the slip.

*   *   *

Stories of other wild animals on the loose in Rome continued throughout the year. Apparently, penguins, snakes and monkeys were rife in the streets. It was obvious that something had to be done when, on the fashionable Parioli Boulevard, a kangaroo was knocked over by a car. One middle-aged Roman became known for persistently driving through the city centre in his open-topped Alfa Romeo. So far so good. But no one looked at his flash car – they were too busy staring at the leopard sitting in the passenger seat. Another Roman, a butcher, kept a lion quietly in his backyard. A former customer revealed the existence of the secret den when the lion bit a child, and the animal was put down.

*   *   *

One Italian journalist was sent to investigate a family of wild pet lovers from whose house, it was rumoured, visitors left with serious injuries. Intent on getting a scoop, the journalist was instead badly mauled. Another Italian gentleman did a favour for a friend on holiday by feeding his lion. It turned out to be a slightly bigger favour than he had in mind – the lion killed him.

* * *

A bar in New Zealand serves a live goldfish cocktail for £3. The Route 66 unhappy hour speciality, 'Goldfish Laybacks' is an attempt to appeal, presumably, to the already very-drunk-indeed market. It consists of tequila, lemon juice and a small Chinese carp.

* * *

In 1992, the Japanese village of Kisakata was invaded by flocks of crop-eating crows. In order to stop the birds from eating all the rice and soy bean crops, the townsfolk started killing about 200 of the birds each month. The problem arose, however, of how to dispose of the bodies. The sharp-minded authorities, always on the look-out for a money-making scheme, decided to try and turn crow into a local delicacy. They set up tasting tests, in which they offered pieces of finely sliced fried beef, lamb, pork and crow to resident gourmets. In the event, only 4 out of the 11 tasters identified the crow from the other meats, and the authorities thought they were on to a winner. Unfortunately, many people were a bit upset with the idea and complained, so Project Crow was scrapped. The problem of what to do with the hundreds of crow corpses was soon solved by people in the neighbouring village, who had discovered that the feathers made rather good lacquer brushes. Thus, instead of appearing as dish of the day, the dead crows were passed on, free of charge, to grateful new owners.

*   *   *

Mexican businessman Bernard Pasquel was determined that his lioness Elsa should not have a dog's life. He started by buying her a leather sofa so that she could recline at her leisure. After a hard day doing, well, nothing at all, Elsa would seek rest in the sanctuary of her large pink circular bed. Concerned that his pet should not have to worry unduly about the basics in life, the businessman also hired a butler to see to Elsa's every need, and each morning he would bath her and spray her with scent, before trotting off to prepare her meals.

*　　*　　*

A South African, accused in court of slaughtering a penguin, said he did it in self-defence because he had never seen such a creature before – and thought it was a 'killer chicken' when it started pecking at his leg on a beach. Mr Nimrod Nbini, 76, then took it home to eat – with killer potatoes and two veg, one imagines ...

*　　*　　*

A Thai villager, Samorn Chanaharn, was arrested selling her two daughters to a brothel to pay for a buffalo.

*　　*　　*

One American magazine which specialized in pets, issued a warning to readers to halt the practice of kissing parrots on their beaks. The warning came as a result of what the magazine described as 'some ugly pecking incidents'.

*   *   *

For the 150 members of the Thames and Chiltern Herpetological Society, owning a regular cat or dog lacks a certain exotic something. So they make pets of reptiles, and are so keen on them that they bring their scaly and slithery friends to society meetings in a community hall. One member, Roland Little, regularly brought along his 15-foot boa constrictor. He also kept 10 snakes in his bedsit, and explained that the landlord was quite OK about them, just as long as Roland didn't invest in anything bigger than a python. Roland's greatest achievement to date had been to breed a family of 21 tiny snakes, which is all the more commendable since snakes are not renowned for their huge libido. Roland was not yet aware of the genders off his baby snakes. He said, 'I have to take them to an expert to be "probed" and they're still a bit small for that. Unfortunately, having their private parts interfered with is not something snakes relish. One sulked at the insult and went off her food for 3 weeks afterwards.'

Robert Snowdon is a committee member of the T and CHS. He admitted that during their get-togethers, there had to be strict rules about how near the pets could get to one another. Robert explained: 'We do have to be careful not to let snakes and lizards sit too close to each other. To say they might not get on is an understatement!' Robert himself keeps lizards. Not only do they need temperatures of 95 degrees, but they also have a penchant for dog food during their carnivorous period. Rob also used to keep over 30 different kinds of frogs, but had to cut back on those when their feeding bills became too high. Instead he keeps snakes, to which he gives highly original names such as Female 1, and Female 2, Male 1 and Male 2. Unfortunately, not everyone shares his love of serpents. His wife apparently can't stand them.

*   *   *

Chris and Trev Hayward from Chelmsford in Essex are the proud owners of 16 snakes. From a 10-foot python to some Indonesian red-tipped tree racers, they all live in a specially adapted cupboard in the Haywards' front hall. The couple regard snakes as relaxation-inducing creatures. 'After a hard day, you can just come home and pick up a snake – like some people have worry beads,' says Trev. Apart from this stress relief role, Chris also explains that snakes are a secure financial investment. If you buy a snake for your child for £15, he reasons, by the time the child leaves home the creature will have grown in value (as well as size) and could be worth hundreds. 'You never lose money on snakes,' says Chris.

*   *   *

In 1992 in Japan, grazing cattle were treated to ghettoblasters in an amazing attempt to help shepherds. Researchers hoped that cows would be receptive enough to be taught to move with music. These animal behaviour specialists believed that if conditioned, cattle would return to their sheds when music was played and so reduce the work of the ranchers. Experiments were conducted during which researchers would feed 16 cattle for 10 days on their favourite feed. After feeding, the cows were serenaded with a rendition of a children's song played on a piano. Later, when the cows were put out to pasture, the same tune was played once more. Researchers watched as all the cattle responded to the music. Indeed, every cow within 200 metres of the entertainment ambled over to the feeding place. Later, the researchers tried the same experiment, but played a different melody. The results were just the same – at the sound of music all the cows congregated at their troughs. Researchers also had to work out the best places to put speakers in the field, and how many would be sufficient for a field of pasture. Officials remarked that the results were better than they had hoped for. They also revealed that another experiment, whereby electronic collar pagers were attached to cows to see if they would react to signals, was in progress. Dial-a-dairy and the bovine version of *Come Dancing* look certain to follow shortly.

* * *

Tom Atwell is the owner of Burke and Hare, two 5-foot-long African dwarf crocodiles. Tom reports that the crocs like to scurry across the carpet and sit quietly on his lap to watch TV. But the duo were mortally terrified of ... the cat. So scared that they would scuttle off snappily as soon as it appeared.

* * *

The council at Henley-on-Thames believes that the sex life of all its residents, but especially of toads, is sacrosanct. That is why they built a special toad-tunnel under a busy road. Before the tunnel was built, the toads were being run over in their hundreds as they hopped across the street to reach their spawning ground.

* * *

A Nottingham family bought a house complete with a beautiful garden and a pond. When they discovered a sweet little lone terrapin in the pond, they took pity on it and went out to buy some more terrapins to keep it company. Sadly, the terrapin was not a terrapin. It was a psychopathic turtle that thought its supposed new pond-mates were not only cute but also looked scrumptious. It ate the lot.

* * *

In 1992, pet expert Mary Brackner warned owners of invertebrates such as cockroaches, spiders, stick insects and worms to make friends with their creepy-crawlies. Lack of such empathy could cause anorexia, lethargy and behavioural changes in pets, warned retired vet Mary, President of the British Small Animal Veterinary Association. The association boasts 3,300 members and Mary believes the interest in creepy-crawlies could be due to the fact that children find them 'more interesting than cats and dogs'. She added, 'When you are close to a member of your family you can tell when they are feeling off-colour. Invertebrates are the same as mammals. You can have the same rapport.'

* * *

Pet-owners in the Yorkshire steel town of Rotherham have an unlikely penchant for the exotic. Pets like red-knee tarantulas and pythons seem to be as common as traditional moggies and whippets. Luckily, one local vet, Mr Lance Jepson, is an expert in pretentious pets. A dab hand at spotting an unwell leech or a sickly spider, his medical repertoire extends even to the complicated procedure of dealing with a tarantula's ruptured stomach – he just sticks it together with glue. Although constantly exposed to exotic animals, Mr Jepson is still surprised by some owners' antics. He comments, 'I never found anyone like the bloke in Rotherham who walked round with a python draped round him, or the woman who slept with her tortoises. All this on top of spiders . . . how the world turns.'

*   *   *

In Pennsylvania, one husband sought divorce from his snake-mad wife because, he claimed, every time he made any amorous advances, she would wrap a huge black snake round her neck to ward him off. In 1969, another American woman had sought a divorce from a husband because of his love for boa constrictors. In her case, it wasn't only the fact that he slept with his 5-foot snakes wrapped around him that ruined a perfectly good marriage. It was more the fact that they were allowed to devour their live mice at the dinner table which really upset her. The judge saw her point: divorce granted.

*   *   *

Graphic designer Ron Brown of Chingford, east London, suffered quietly for over 30 years as his wife filled their house with sick birds. Teacher Anita, known locally as the Birdwoman of Chingford, kept as many as 80 birds in the house. The last straw for Ron was when she brought a stricken jackdaw into their bedroom beause she felt it needed company. He was citing unreasonable behaviour in the divorce case early in 1993.

*   *   *

A 68-year-old Yorkshire woman was granted a divorce on the grounds that her husband never slept with her. Instead he spent the night with the great love of his life – his horse, Trigger.

*   *   *

When Dolly Duffin died in 1990, she left her affairs in good order. Her niece Susan Kirkwood received £350 and some photographs. Dolly had even remembered to provide for her tortoise, Fred. She left him £26,000. Dolly's devotion to her hard-shelled friend was already legendary in Hull, for Dolly would take him shopping perched on her sholder or, during his hibernation, wrapped up in blankets in a push-chair. The RSPCA in charge of the trust fund paid Mrs Kirkwood 50p per week to keep Fred in the manner to which he was accustomed – namely in a Fortnum and Mason tea-chest with lettuce and water for tasty snacks. Fred was only 35 and could have lived up to 100. Mrs Kirkwood bore no resentment that Fred got the lump sum. She said simply, 'We will not miss what we never had, so we are not upset.'

*   *   *

In 1988, the American people held their breath over the fate of Whitey, a 9-year-old carriage horse who had collapsed from heat-exhaustion in the street. After being hosed down, massaged and fed pain-killers and, no doubt, inspired by the huge crowds that had gathered, Whitey eventually managed to get up and be led to the sanctuary of his stable. Over the next few days, the health of Whitey overshadowed all other major news events. There were daily bulletins on his progress, offers from several people who wanted to buy him and politicians called press conferences and promised stricter laws on cab horses working in hot weather. Finally, the whole nation breathed a sigh of relief as Whitey departed for a month's farm holiday.

*   *   *

Rita Stratta, recently retired pet buyer for Harrods, revealed that in the 36 years of working there she had received some pretty bizarre requests. One customer had asked for a camel with 3 humps, whilst one of the top universities had tried asking for a pterodactyl. But Rita was ready for such a ruse. A novel variant on the standard: 'Sorry, sir, they're out of stock,' she told them to try elsewhere. On another occasion, a gentleman wanted to send a gift to his ex-wife to mark her re-marriage, and asked Rita to send a skunk. Rita followed his wishes but added, 'I thought it was a bit off, because the animal was terribly smelly.'

* * *

In 1992, fish-lover Peter Dashwood from Shirley in Southampton tried a new technique to stop the neighbours' cats from disturbing his pets. Peter, who had turned his garden into a haven for fish, frogs and newts, had tried 'every trick in the book' to stop local cats from eating his best koi and mirror carp. So, when all else failed, he lured the moggies into a trap with tins of herrings and then deported them. He would drive the cats miles away from home and then abandon them. He dealt with 5 felines in this manner and would have carried on, if his neighbours hadn't become suspicious and ordered an investigation by the RSPCA. One neighbour, Mrs Sandra Spencer, who had had 3 of her cats mysteriously disappear The Dashwood Way, remained unmoved by his claims that he'd only done it because he hated seeing his fish killed. She retorted, 'How can anyone call himself an animal lover and then do this kind of thing to pets and their owners?' Defending his actions, Mr Dashwood, a ferry bosun, said, 'I knew what I was doing was wrong, but I was very frustrated. I never harmed the cats and always hoped they would be found and looked after by someone else.' Mr Dashwood claimed that he had dismantled a wire trap and had now decided to invest in a sonic radar system to try and keep the cats at bay.

* * *

In 1992, the pot-bellied pig was superseded by that other exotic animal – the fainting goat. This is a creature that has been made neurotic through in-breeding ... So neurotic, in fact, that it goes stiff and topples over at the faintest noise or shock. The publisher of *Exotic*

Breeds Journal promised: 'They are a growing pet trend. You'll see more people wanting them.' There is even a Fainting Goat Association in Nebraska. To become a member you have to provide photographic evidence of your goat in mid-collapse, which is graded from 1 to 6, 6 being the most dramatic swoon.

*   *   *

In 1992, EC regulations threatened to confuse budgie owners; legislation from Brussels meant they would have to license their feathered friends. The ruling would give as much protection to sparrows and starlings as it would to the single spix macaw believed to be left alive. David Neville from the National Aviculture Council suggested that the regulations were excessive for Britain, and whilst they might be effective in protecting endangered species, there was no need to cover the more common birds. It is a different matter in France and Belgium however, where every year, millions of starlings are made into pâté.

*   *   *

In 1984, tennis player Johan Kriek was without

his lucky mascot when he faced John McEnroe in the tennis quarter-finals at Madison Square Gardens. The mascot was Monty, his python, which at 12 months already measured 4 feet. Described as 'still growing and with a keen appetite for mice', Monty was a regular spectator at Kriek's matches. This time, however, the snake had been left at home in Florida because Kriek believed the climate in New York would be unsuitable for him. Kriek's wife Trish admitted that her husband had taken Monty on to the court in his kit bag and that on other occasions she had carried him to her husband's matches in her handbag.

*   *   *

In 1983, bachelor Melvyn Spry got himself into a spot of bother when parts of his business kept going walkies. Mel, from Chard in Somerset, ran a mail order service, sending out various exotic creatures from his home. As might be expected, his neighbours didn't like the idea, especially as one elderly chap in his street, Arthur Pace, had recently found a dead South American rat snake in his kitchen cupboard. As if that wasn't enough, a neighbour on the other side, Mrs Myra Bellamy, discovered a dragon lizard in her son's bed-room. Whilst Mel was applying for permission to turn his home into a pet shop, the council were applying for a nuisance order. In a valiant attempt to defend himself, Mel denied that the rat snake found in Mr Pace's cupboard was one of his.

*　　*　　*

In 1976, van driver Bob Bird saw his best friend George upside down in the fish pond at the bottom of the garden. Pulling George out, Bob administered the kiss of life. After a tense 15 minutes George coughed, spluttered and started to breathe. Bob was so relieved – life without his 21-year-old tortoise would have been miserable. He said, 'George is more than a pet and I was really desperate. The first thing I thought of was the kiss of life.'

*　　*　　*

Joey the pet goldfish was grateful that his owner Mr Shrewring had learnt how to give the kiss of life whilst he was in the Navy. Mr Shrewring, of Chatham in Kent, saw Joey lying lifeless at the bottom of a cracked empty fish bowl. With not a minute to waste, Mr Shrewring held the fish alternately under the hot and cold taps, trying to revive him. When this seemed to have no effect, he gave the goldfish the kiss of life by blowing into its mouth for 15 minutes. It obviously worked, for Joey started to show signs of life, whereupon he was subjected to a further 10 minutes of the hot and cold water treatment ... which no doubt nearly finished him off again.

* * *

Oscar, a 12-year-old goldfish, was inadvertently left outside in his bowl one winter's night and froze solid. He was discovered the next morning by the Butler children, Anne and Catherine, who rushed the rigid fish into their father. John Butler broke the ice and thawed Oscar out in lukewarm water. Then he spent the next hour trying to encourage Oscar's gills to work. Desperate to succeed, John also massaged Oscar's tummy and ingeniously gave him the kiss of life with an eye dropper. Four hours later Oscar was swimming merrily round his bowl again.

* * *

Peter Thawley from Skegness in Lincolnshire found a hedgehog floating in the pond at his parents' home. Rescuing it and putting it by the boiler didn't raise any sign of life, so Peter tried giving it the kiss of life with a bicycle pump. When all else failed, he administered a double brandy. It worked beautifully.

*　　*　　*

Pet-shop owner Peter Dugmore from Wolverhampton gave a falcon a false pair of wings after its own had been clipped too severely. The wings were cleverly crafted by inserting pigeon feathers into the broken stumps of the falcon's own feathers. When the falcon grew new wings, the makeshift ones dropped off during moulting.

*　　*　　*

One American woman treated her baby chimpanzee like a newly born child. Not only did she wheel it around in a pram, but the chimp was treated to his own bed, wardrobe and expensive toys. He was fed gourmet food, and especially liked having his teeth brushed and his hair combed and watching TV. The

monkey even knew what his right arm was for
. . . there was nothing he enjoyed better than a
swift half (of orange juice) with his owner in a
bar.

*   *   *

In 1978, Ron Stirman had an unusual bed
partner in the shape of Jaws, his 4-foot
alligator. Ron, a 25-year-old reptile enthusiast,
explained: 'I quite often have him in my bed
for the night. Alligators need warmth and he
particularly enjoys it during the winter when I
use an electric blanket. He snuggles right
down under the sheets and goes to sleep
immediately.' Alongside Jaws were 3 young
pythons and 2 dwarf crocodiles from Botswana.
Ron, who lived with his parents, admitted that
his mother has refused to go into his bedroom
since one of the crocodiles escaped. Neighbours were also wary of the reptiles. In fact,
they got a protest petition up after Jaws had
tried to snap up next door's cat during an
exercise session in the garden. However, Ron's
girlfriend Pauline Fennings was a little more
understanding and would have a crocodile on
her lap whilst watching the television. Pauline
was less friendly with the snakes, however,

because one of Ron's earlier pets, a 9-foot python had, as Ron put it, 'had a bit of a go at her'. Whilst not trying to eat girlfriends or neighbours' pets, the reptiles enjoyed a diet of fish and mice, which Ron bred himself. This diet cost him £2 per week. The biggest expense was heating, at £36 a quarter. Ron displayed no apprehension about the fact that lovable, fun-loving Jaws would eventually double in length and weigh half a ton. He dismissed all fear by saying, 'He is a very amiable alligator. I can do anything with him. I once even gave him artificial respiration when he got a nasty shock from an electric heater.' Speaking further about their relationship, Ron admitted that behind that great mouth, Jaws was really a bit of a softie: 'I wouldn't say they were terribly affectionate creatures, but Jaws did go right off his food when I was in hospital once.'

*　　*　　*

There was a big demand in the States in the early 1970s for language records ... that is, language records for teaching English, to parrots.

*　　*　　*

A Yorkshire firm specializing in pet gear once received an urgent call from a desperate pet-owner. 'Was there any chance,' asked the caller, 'that the firm could make his 2 goldfish a couple of nice little swimsuits?' Not to be defeated, the firm soon had 2 miniature blue-and-white striped silk swimsuits on their way to the prize-winning goldfish. The reason for the request had nothing to do with fashion, but the fact that the fish were being treated for a fungus with cream and the owner wanted to prevent them from rubbing it off on the side of the fishbowl.

*   *   *

In 1964 in America you could hire a pet for the summer. For £175 per day, you could have a fully-grown elephant in your garden, complete with handler. For the same amount, you could enjoy the company of a lion, but for those who didn't wish to spend so much, a leopard, tiger or camel could be yours for just £80 per day. Those who think these prices were a bit hot will be relieved to know that at the end of the summer half the money was refunded – if the animal was returned in good condition. Mr Henry Trefflich, the firm's owner, revealed that one of his customers was a Long Island society hostess who felt that her parties lacked that certain *je ne sais quoi* if there wasn't a camel or an ape tethered near the bar. Another fashion at high-society parties was to hire half a dozen baby elephants, which were all duly painted pink.

* * *

A 12-foot-long hungry python couldn't believe his luck when he was left alone in a house with just a 9-year-old boy for company. Feeling a trifle peckish, the python started to get friendly and wrapped himself round Alex Henry at his home in Long Beach, California. A fire department spokesman confirmed that the python was indeed trying to swallow the boy. Not that anyone needed much convincing . . . when the ambulancemen arrived the snake already had its chops around the lad's foot.

* * *

When a 6-foot boa constrictor was believed to be on the loose in London's sewers, police issued a warning that the snake might appear in bathrooms at whim. Should this happen, the police continued, the public were advised to put the toilet seat down.

*　　*　　*

Chocky the parrot was bequeathed £10,000 by his late owner, which was used to keep him in grapes, fruit cake and parrot feed until he died. Chocky also had the rare privilege of being given a perch in the same aviary as Sir John Gielgud's parrot. Knowing how faithfully talking birds copy their owner's vocabulary, how sad it was that one bird, well known at the time in Tenby, could not have moved into the same cage. The Welsh parrot's only phrase was, 'Show us your knickers, then.'

4

Some Pets Do 'Ave Em
. . . The Things People Do
with their Animals . . .
and Animals with their People

A cable company in Columbia, South Carolina put out several days of 24-hour live coverage of a fish tank as a test transmission before they began broadcasting their proper programmes. When they stopped the fish show, however, they received thousands of complaints from viewers saying they preferred watching fish. The aquarium was consequently given its own show, which goes out for 14 hours every day and is pulling in high ratings.

*   *   *

Steve Partridge of Sherborne, Dorset was on his way to his regular Sunday football game when, tragically, he ran over the family terrier Jacko in the drive. Pulling forward to free the dog, he ran over and killed Chivers, the family's other pet. Steve, a plasterer, stopped to comfort his wife and children, but it was decided, even with 2 dead pets, that he should go to the match. He arrived late, and at the end of the game gave away a penalty – earning the opposition a 1–1 draw!

*   *   *

Japanese electronics company Takara came up with the perfect pet in 1992. Their cat, originally named Mew, purred when stroked, was guaranteed never to be sick, never to be hungry and certainly never to be responsible for any unsightly messes on your carpet. Costing £52, Mew sold an amazing 78,000 in the first 3 months, mostly to young single females. The fake pets' increasingly popularity was believed to be a result of the loneliness of people living in inner cities – and the refusal by most landlords to allow real pets. A spokesman from Takara said, 'We believe Mew is the ultimate pet.'

* * *

In 1990, a survey by the Royal Society for the Prevention of Accidents concluded that 1 in every 100 mishaps in the home was caused by pets. One man for example, fell and sprained his ankle when he stood on a chair to try and catch his budgie. Similarly, a woman toppled over and broke her foot whilst attempting to get her budgie back into its cage. Perhaps the most bizarre misadventure was that of the woman who was injured while she tried to prevent the family moggie from running off with the Sunday roast. The Royal Society also warned against smaller pets such as hamsters and guinea pigs who, they said, could show sudden spurts of speed, causing their owners to fall whilst in hot pursuit. Most accidents, though, were caused by owners simply falling over their pets. So the Society recommended that stairways were well lit and that feeding bowls were kept out of the main walkways inside houses.

* * *

Arthur Ling, president of the Vegan Society, was deposed after he committed a cardinal sin

– he killed a mouse. Vegans eat no animals or animal products at all. Owner of a soya milk factory, Arthur was caught by Animal Liberation Front activists within the Vegan Society setting a mousetrap, albeit one baited with vegan cheese. When Oxford vegan Philip Brown stood up at a meeting to defend Arthur, things got worse. Sharp-eyed activists noticed he was wearing leather shoes and howled him down with cries of, 'Your shoes are an act of violence.' Police were called to stand by in case of further trouble.

*   *   *

In Japan, despite the recession, Kyon was having a ball. She regularly dined on the tastiest gourmet food, dressed in designer clothes, had a health care plan and indulged in her once-a-month beauty regime at the local parlour. In return for all these perks, Kyon didn't even have to lift a finger – or rather, a paw. Kyon was one of the thousands of pampered Japanese pets who live the life of Riley. One pet shop in Tokyo offers pet weddings so that, if the fancy took her, Kyon could tie the knot with the hound of her dreams. Such a wedding would set her back

£200, but for this amount the groomhound would get a morning suit and the bridebitch would get a white satin wedding dress. Michiko Kimura, who runs the wedding service and presides over the ceremony, added, 'To the Japanese, a pet is just like a member of the family, so they want to give it the best.' And if all this high living should cause your pet stress, a Tokyo therapist has the answer. Shigenori Masuda, who runs a smart dog-grooming parlour in the city, claims to relieve cats and dogs of their stress with special yoga exercises. Every month he pulls, twists and turns between 30 and 100 animals into shape. It looks quite bizarre, Dr Masuda often stretching animals above his head, but apparently this helps them to relax. Indeed, the dogs and cats seem positively serene during their yoga workouts.

*   *   *

The largest ever survey of pets' names was carried out by the RSPCA in 1991. The animal organization conducted a poll amongst 400,000 young people as part of National Pet Week. As well as charting trends in pets' names, the survey also concluded that, when it came down to it, the British were rather unimaginative. For example, the top name for dogs was Ben, the top name for cats was Sooty and the top title for goldfish was Jaws. The poll also revealed that classic favourites such as Fido and Rover had, as it were, gone to the dogs. Mr David Graham, the RSPCA's senior education officer, said he had expected to find more dogs named Prince, but in fact 'they are really numerous only in places like Surrey, where people seem more interested in the royal family'. The poll also confirmed the suspicion that, like fast cars, big dogs were used as an indication of their owners' supposed virility. Hence many city animals, no doubt even some poodles, responded to the call of Rocky, Tyson and Bruno. Mr Graham was also perturbed at what seemed like an outbreak of unkindness when it came to naming goldfish. He explained, 'A lot of them have quite nasty names like Fish and Chips.' The names Fred and George proved to be incredibly popular across the whole range of pets. Mr Graham interpreted this as a profound reflection of our attitudes towards our 4-legged friends by pointing out, quite reasonably, that 'they are not very popular, indeed slightly silly names with humans'. On being asked why the British were so unimaginative when it came to bestowing their pets with a title, Mr Graham showed remarkable insight. He said sagely 'When it comes down to it, the Englishman doesn't want to stick out. No one wants to stand on a doorstep shouting, "Come in Archimedes!" '

Favourite Names for Pets in Britain 1991:
Dogs: 1–Ben, 2–Sam, 3–Lady, 4–Max, 5–Sheba.
Cats: 1–Sooty, 2–Tigger, 3–Tiger, 4–Smokey, 5–Ginger.
Goldfish: 1–Jaws, 2–Goldie, 3–Fred, 4–Tom, 5–Bubbles.
Rabbits: 1–Snowy, 2–Thumper, 3–Flopsy, 4–Sooty, 5–Smokey.
Budgies: 1–Joey, 2–Billy, 3–Bluey, 4–Bobby, 5–Snowy.
Guinea Pigs: 1–Squeak, 2–Ginger, 3–Bubbles, 4–Patch, 5–Snowy.
Hamsters: 1–Hammy, 2–Honey, 3–Harry, 4–Fluffy, 5–Bubbles.
Gerbils: 1–Squeak, 2–Jerry, 3–Bubble, 4–Tom, 5–Snowy.
Tortoises: 1–Speedy, 2–Fred, 3–Tommy, 4–Toby, 5–Terry.
Rats: 1–Ratty, 2–Roland, 3–Splinter, 4–Ben, 5–Squeak.

Ponies: 1–Copper, 2–Beauty, 3–Bramble, 4–Star, 5–Misty.
Mice: 1–Mickey, 2–Squeak, 3–Jenny, 4–Minnie, 5–Speedy.

* * *

Scentchips were pet fresheners marketed to neutralize the nastier niffs created by pets. If your poodle was suffering from flatulence or your cat had bad breath, you could create a more fragrant atmosphere with these air fresheners which came in various scents, such as mountain laurel, vanilla, watermelon and wild cherry.

* * *

Do you have a podgy poodle or a corpulent cat? Don't worry. The latest product is low-calorie pet food. Available on prescription only. Pets with halitosis, meanwhile, have the ideal solution in Chew-eez, the gum for dogs. It promises better teeth, better gums and fresher breath.

* * *

A Southampton firm called Restapet specialized in pet coffins. As an advert for their
services, this ditty was composed: 'Your pet
has been a pal to you/Deserving all the
comfort due/Whether its coat is smooth or
rough/There will come a time when he's had
enough.' Reports that pets died laughing at
this are as yet unconfirmed.

*　　*　　*

A survey done by the RSPCA in 1990 found
there were geographical trends when it came
to keeping a pet. Their survey, which involved
10,000 youngsters, revealed that young people
in Wales were more likely to keep dogs; there
were more budgies in the north; more ponies
in the south-west and more hamsters in the
south-east. One shock result concerned that
most dynamic of pets, the stick insect. It only
narrowly missed being in the top ten list of
most popular pets.

*　　*　　*

In 1992, a Japanese bank introduced a pet
account service, which allowed money-
minded pets to save just as much as their

owners. The bank, Sanwa, the sixth largest in Japan, said that the new service was a result of requests from customers who wanted to treat their pets as members of the family. Thus, 3 different types of pet accounts were offered. Spokesman Atsushi Chikamochi said that the service would help owners in the expensive activity of keeping a pet. The bank's own research showed that owners spent Y6,000 (£40) taking their pets to the vet, whilst a visit to a beauty parlour could cost £70. Spokesman Chikamochi also stressed that the accounts were open to all types of pets.

*　　*　　*

In New York, political correctness deemed it essential for the term 'pet' (which was considered somewhat patronizing) to be replaced with the description 'companion animal'.

*　　*　　*

Millie, the best-selling author and spaniel belonging to George Bush, was given an accolade by her master the President during the 1992 election campaign. 'Millie,' asserted Bush, 'knows more about foreign policy than those two bozos Bill Clinton and Al Gore.'

* * *

The Long Island Pet Cemetery Scandal outraged many pet lovers. The owners of the
cemetery had apparently not carried out indi-
vidual burial or cremation of pets as promised.
Instead, they were burying them in communal
graves or cremating them *en masse*. This heart-
less practice only came to light after a budgie
owner received his dead pet's ashes ... The
package contained a dog's tooth.

* * *

A professor at Columbia University, Renee
Solomon, got herself in a spot of bother over
some pigeons. Her next-door neighbours in
her Manhattan skyscraper were the Epsteins,
who happened to be bird lovers. And, being
bird lovers, they regularly left bird seed on
their terrace for their feathered friends. So far
so good ... until Professor Solomon started to
be woken in the early hours by short-sighted
pigeons bashing into her windows in their
search for the seed. The pigeons then started
to roost on her window-sill, leaving their

droppings behind in substantial amounts. Prof. Solomon was not best pleased, and sent the Epsteins a note informing them of her problem. Unfortunately the birds still kept on coming. Things came to a head when Professor Solomon returned home one day to find bullet holes in her window. The bullets had been fired by other disgruntled residents who were also infuriated by the birds and were trying their own methods of discouraging them. At the end of her tether, Professor Solomon called the building superintendent, who tried to help out by smearing her window-sill with a pigeon-repelling gel. This action annoyed the Epsteins, who informed the American Society for the Protection of Birds and they sent an officer round to investigate. The officer, Mr Hernandez, concluded that the gel was too thick and therefore a threat to smaller birds. After this, Professor Solomon received threatening calls from both the Epsteins and Mr Hernandez. Then, whilst she was away on holiday, the American Society for the Prevention of Cruelty to Animals raided her flat to take pictures of her window-sills. The whole affair came to boiling point when Professor Solomon, sitting quietly in her university study, was arrested by a group of policemen accompanied by Mr Hernandez. Outraged, Professor Solomon kicked one of the policemen on the shins and was subsequently charged with killing birds *and* resisting arrest, handcuffed and locked up. The charges were finally dropped, but Professor Solomon didn't want to let it rest there. Last thing we heard, she was suing her neighbours and the city for wrongful arrest, false imprisonment and slander.

*   *   *

In 1990, Parisian artist Thierry Poncelet got fed up with restoring family portraits. It was, he felt, a waste of his genius. So one day, as he was touching up an old portrait of an unattractive woman, he painted a dog's head over her face, then set the finished picture in his window with a price tag of £600. To his amazement, it sold. Not only did that one sell, but so did a whole host of others. Thierry turned distant relatives into spaniels, pussycats and poodles. A flood of aristocratic customers approached, and asked him to do special commissions. Thierry complied; his work increased and so did his prices. The customer who claimed that his pet poodle was reminiscent of the Mona Lisa paid £1,000 to have his point proved.

Thierry even did a portrait of a monkey in Napoleon's uniform, complete with a banana sticking out of his pocket. In fact, his paintings became so popular that, at an exhibition soon afterwoods, 35 out of the 50 portraits were sold. Thierry takes all the interest in his stride. When he put his fees up to £2,000, the commissions still kept on rolling in. 'I tell you,' he says, 'all artists are mad. But the customers are crazier still.'

*　　*　　*

A Japanese survey discovered that owners spent twice as much money on dogs as they did on cats. Two-thirds of dog owners admitted to spending money on the beautification of their mutts, whilst a disappointing 6 out of 10 cat owners said they didn't spend a single yen on making their moggie look more presentable. One in 10 of the people questioned also spent Y14,000 on hotels for their pets whilst they themselves went on holiday.

*　　*　　*

Research in several parts of the world suggests that owning a pet can bring down blood pressure, reduce heart disease, provide stimulation for the old, the young – and the criminally inclined. A prison in Switzerland has introduced cats to the cells, not to keep the mice down, but to make prisoners happy and give them a sense of responsibility. And at Garth Prison in Lancashire, prisoners have taken to keeping birds. Research showed that more than 80 long-term inmates kept pets, mostly feathered, but also farm animals. Mary Whyham, senior probation officer at the prison, extolled the virtues of pets. She claimed that pet-keeping resulted in making those behind bars less violent; security problems, medication and suicide rates were also reduced. At Garth, more than 85 budgerigars and cockatiels were kept in cells whilst their owners attended pet-care classes. An Edinburgh prison has taken pet-keeping one step further. Inmates there are breeding fish (which are high in protein) which they intend to send to the hungry in Third World countries.

*　　*　　*

In 1991, CDs of relaxing music for cats and dogs went on sale in Japan. The result of 20 years of research by Japanese vet, Dr Norio Aoki, the

CD for canines included harmonies such as 'Woody Dance' and 'Daydreaming in the Wood'. Cats (those with a CattoBlaster, of course) could mellow out to tunes such as 'Nice Pine Forest' and 'Events in a Strange Forest'. Dr Aoki's quest was to help pets relax when in the strange environment of a clinic. He carried out exhaustive testing with tracks ranging from Chopin to the Sex Pistols. Taking notes of the pets' reactions – from the flickering of their pupils to the flapping of their ears – helped the vet to isolate the most effective music. Just to be on the safe side, he also subjected the animals to what was no doubt the highly-stressful experience of being wired to encephalograms to measure their brainwaves, electrocardiograms to measure their heart rhythms, and X-rays to check the reponses of their colons to music. A total of 10,000 copies of the pet CDs sold in the first few months.

*   *   *

In 1992, car salesman Tom Ireland offered not part-exchange but pet-exchange deals. Pet lovers Tom and his wife Maureen from Northumberland accepted pets instead of old bangers from their customers. One happy customer swapped 2 Rottweiler pups as part-payment for a Range Rover. Budgies, pot-bellied pigs and tom-cats also changed hands. Now the couple have a collection of 1 donkey, 2 emus, 2 ponies, 4 pigs and 5 dogs. Tom said, 'We love animals. So if a customer does not have a car we'll take a pet.' Tom has yet to be offered a cheetah – the ultimate nice little runner.

*   *   *

Well, you can get credit terms for everything else, so why not pets? Maureen Smith of Animal Fayre in Hereford offers some of her more expensive pets on the never-never. Prices for a koi carp, for example, started at £2,000 and hit the ceiling at £12,000. Other pricey pets include zebra catfish (£2,300) a Mississippi paddle fish (£1,000), cockatoos (up to £2,000) and champion cats and dogs (as much as £5,000). When it comes to talking birds such as parrots and budgies, a rude vocabulary can triple the asking price. An African grey parrot who said, 'Who's a pretty boy then?' cost £650, but a similar parrot who could squawk, 'Not that bloody woman again!' would set you back £2,500. Maureen added, 'Perhaps we should be offering second mortgages as well as HP.'

*   *   *

In 1988, a Plymouth man walked out on his wife ... and her snakes, frogs, lizards and iguanas. He just couldn't stand them any more. Another man from Cornwall sought a divorce from his wife because she travelled 6 miles in a taxi every morning to get fresh fish for her cat – but never once made breakfast for him.

*   *   *

Dallas travel agent Ed Lang dreamed up the perfect holiday for pampered pets. For only £700, they got a week's cruise up the Mississippi on board the American Cruiselines ship *New Orleans*, whilst their owners accompanied them free of charge. The pets enjoyed 4-star service with *haute cuisine* meals, free run of the ship – and special staff on hand to clear up any deposits left on the, err, poop deck ...

*   *   *

In 1987, Francesca Findlater, the director of a

London company called Pretentious Pets, came up with the ultimate gifts for spoiled pets. Moving on from their Santa Claus suits, especially tailored for dogs, Francesca floated the idea of a personal portfolio for all those pets interested in stocks and shares. The shares – a minimum of £100 – would of course have been invested in relevant companies such as Spillers, the makers of Winalot.

*   *   *

Psychic experts believe that pets can sense future events, especially dangerous ones. Also in their range of ESP skills is their ability to perceive beings that the human eyes cannot see and even read their owners' thoughts telepathically. Barbara Woodhouse recalled an incident when, whilst playing polo, she was struck in the mouth by a ball. Without having been able to see what had happened, and without even stopping, her horse rushed her straight over to the first aid tent.

*   *   *

During a televised election debate in 1988, President Mitterand and Jacques Chirac fell

out over that great political debate – pet food.
Chirac pointed out that as Mayor of Paris and a
citizen he had to protest over the fact that the
President had imposed VAT to be doubled on
food for dogs and cats. Without flinching,
Mitterand protested, 'You do not have a
monopoly of affection for cats and dogs. I love
them as much as anybody.'

*   *   *

In 1989, the cats and dogs of France ate their
way through more meat than the entire popu-
lation of Spain.

*   *   *

In 1991, a new superstore opened in a Parisian
suburb. Mille Amis looked like your average
Prisunic from the outside, but once inside
shoppers discovered that the £3 million
complex had been dedicated entirely to pets.
Whilst *Madame* or *Monsieur* chose doggy's
dinner from an exotic range, their poodle
could enjoy a massage and hair-do. Alterna-
tively, pets could browse at leisure in any
department which took their fancy: 'Health

and Fitness', 'Relaxation', Beauty' and 'Education and Reading'.

*   *   *

In 1989, a psychologist set up a telephone helpline in Dublin for grieving owners who had lost their pets. Ms Aine Wellard, 32, who pioneered the free service, reported that in the first few months 53 people had called for help. Ms Wellard claims that people who have lost their pets may be unwilling to admit to the extent of their grief. 'If someone is alone and the budgie is all they talk to every day, it will be like missing a relative'. To back her theory, Ms Wellard cited the example of a woman who took her sick dog to the vet, where it died. The woman was so upset that she took the dog's bowl and lead and put them on the back seat of the car. That in itself is not too odd, but, as Ms Wellard pointed out, 'Keeping a dog lead as a memento is one thing, but when you can't put shopping on the back seat in case you disturb a dog bowl, that's another.'

*   *   *

In 1984, there was a furore when health service union officials found that various family pets, a cow and a racehorse had all been treated on the NHS. It was discovered that vets had referred these pets to 'moonlighting' hospital consultants for blood tests in NHS laboratories. Three vets in the Derby area had been passing on this extra work to consultants, and were only found out when sharp-eyed lab assistants noticed the pets' name on the bottles.

*　　*　　*

In 1985, Don Milton started a Canine and Feline Butler Service. Don, from Richmond in Surrey, soon had 60 4-legged clients on his books. Whilst their owners were away, Don would visit cats in the afternoon, leaving food, changing litter trays and providing fresh water. Rates weren't too bad either; to feed up to 4 cats, Don charged just £3.00. Dogs were a different matter as they required more visits, because, as Don said, 'They easily succumb to boredom'. Dog visits cost 50p more. Don claimed he knew there was a demand for his services, because of all the dejected pets he had picked up from kennels in his pet taxi service, which had been running successfully for the previous 3 years. Don started up with a

£90 van and £3.50 cash in hand. He charged £12.50 each way for a kennel trip or £12.50 for a visit to the vet, where he waited until the pet had been treated and took it home in the comfort of the chauffeur-driven van. Don admitted that his workload was forcing him to train selected people to help out. But he added, 'They must be of a high calibre and I look for references going back 8 years.'

*   *   *

In 1988, it was estimated that 61 per cent of American households had 1 or more pets, the highest proportion in the world. American congressmen received more mail about animal issues than any other subject. The nation's most popular pet was the humble, low maintenance fish, on whose upkeep Americans spend £135 million a year. In Britain the pet ownership figure is around 51 per cent with 5.8 million dogs, 4.7 million cats and just under a million budgies. A survey for *Options* magazine revealed that 1 in 10 pet-owners preferred their furry, feathered or finned friends to their spouses. Half the people questioned valued their pet above money, a fifth said they were more important than children and a third admitted that they would rather give up work than lose their animal.

* * *

The Centre for the Interaction of Animals and Society in the States reported that 99 per cent of dog and cat owners regularly chat to their pets. A further 40 per cent go the whole hog by carrying their pet's photo in their wallet and celebrating their birthdays.

* * *

In 1989, obituaries for pets started to appear in a new column in the *Pennsylvanian Daily Local News*. Not just a declaration of the pet's demise, these obituaries also included some of the beast's finest hours, traits or habits. The column, which appeared weekly and covered half a page, was the first of its kind, and reverently named 'Pause To Remember', or irreverently, 'Paws To Remember'. One such tribute was to Quanah, a pedigree Doberman, which had been placed by Mrs Pam Gutekunst. She described her sorely-missed hound as 'a show dog who loved to entertain the masses'. Similarly, Noel the guinea-pig was mourned by all the children at St Joseph's Kindergarten.

Struck down in his prime, Noel was lovingly remembered by teacher Mrs Maryellen Coombe as a fun-loving pet: 'He used to run around on the floor during reading time and would sometimes squeal at the most inopportune moments.' The newspaper's editor, Mr David Warner, said he was surprised at the amount of interest the obituaries had generated, and defended them as 'the stuff of human interest'. Mr Dave Spadaro, a sports writer on the *Daily Local News* was less impressed. Obviously not a man sympathetic to such remembrances, he called the column 'a slap in the face of intelligence'.

*   *   *

The RSPCA's summer report of 1987 declared that pet breeders who tinkered with nature to provide fashion-conscious owners with an aesthetical pet were misguided and cruel. The breeders' attempts to produce Pekinese, Boxer and English bulldogs with shorter noses could, claimed the RSPCA, lead to respiratory problems for the dogs. The trend for producing animals to order started in America, where a designer cat was marketed just in time for Christmas. This festive feline had been specially bred to look like a diminutive version of a large wild cat. It was advertised as the ideal pet to blend in with jungle print wallpaper. Mr Tony Self, head of the clinical veterinary services, said curtly, 'One can only hope that the price tag of $1,400 will successfully kill that particular piece of nonsense.'

*   *   *

In 1978, a spiritualist called Vera amazed locals with her abilities to trace missing pets. When Vera, from Hornsea in Humberside, was called in by the RSPCA for help, she would meditate for a few moments and then drift off into a deep trance. Whilst in the trance, Vera would draw a detailed picture of where the missing pet was to be found. One of Vera's successes involved a valuable Siamese cat called Sasha. In her trance, Vera drew a garden shed with a broken drainpipe, which she said was less than a mile away. After searching with a friend, Vera found the exact shed with Sasha inside. A further example of Vera's psychic powers was shown when she advised her friend Mrs Schofield not to buy the Labrador that she wanted because she would soon have more than she could handle. Sure enough, soon

afterwards, Mrs Schofield found herself looking after no less than 5 stray Labradors, all of
whom had turned up out of the blue, needing a
kennel for the night.

*　　*　　*

Americans who couldn't afford expensive pets
in the 60s were offered ... an Executive Ant
Farm for about £4.

*　　*　　*

In 1961, Cardinal Godfrey, the Catholic Arch-
bishop of Westminster, suggested that pets
should take part in Family Fast Days. The
Cardinal drew on a reference from the Bible
which supported his recommendation. The
third chapter of the book of Jonah describes
how the Ninevites, encouraged by the king
and his nobles, tried to avoid impending
disaster with the cry, 'A fast for man and beast'.
Cardinal Godfrey translated Jonah's message
into more modern terms, saying: 'Something
could be saved too in the care of our pets.
They could also benefit by being fed with less
expensive foods.' Getting more specific,
Godfrey suggested that 'a plump and pampered poodle might run all the more gaily after

a reduced diet of simpler fare, and perhaps denied a visit to a hair stylist . . .'

*   *   *

In 1967, a firm in Stockport produced that essential item for the rodent in your life, not mousetraps, but mouse mattresses. This idea was the brainchild of Mr Walter Ellision, who was known as the King of Pet Pamperers. Not only did mice benefit from his schemes, but bulldogs could also don his lemon-coloured silk jackets as they reclined in his foam-filled baskets sporting his pearl necklaces from their jowly necks. As the 100 staff in his 2 Cheshire-based factories worked flat out to provide the pet accessories, Walt claimed proudly: 'By now there must be over 500 dogs lounging about the house in my necklaces. They are the same pearls as used in women's costume jewellery and are rather a specialist line.' Walt, obviously a man of impeccable taste, added, 'I think it is very attractive when the lady of the house is sitting about in her jewellery and her dog is wearing the same.' Oddly enough, dog breeder Mrs Jessie Millet, who owned a bulldog named Hattie, dis-agreed. She explained, 'I'm a dog lover from the dog's point of view. I try to put myself in the dog's place, and think how I would feel.' Musing for a moment, she then added, 'And if anyone put a necklace on me I would bite them . . . ' Sceptics who thought that Walt couldn't make a profit out of his 5,000 different animal beauty aids were shocked by his annual turnover of £1,000,000.

*   *   *

For a period during the Cold War, animal air-raid shelters were all the rage in America. They came complete with atomic fall-out protection and food and drink supplies.

*   *   *

A 20-year-old American girl made her fiancé sign a pet pact. The girl, owner of 2 dogs, 5 cats, a donkey and a pony, was concerned that the animals should enjoy their freedom even after she was married. She got her husband-to-be to agree that the donkey, who slept in a special bed in her room, and her pony, which slept in the stable but had access to the house at all times, would not have their privileges restricted. The young man, obviously blinded by love, agreed to all the terms and hoped that things might change after they were married. Prospects didn't look too good, however, when the bride cut their honeymoon short by 3 days to hurry home to her pets.

*   *   *

Mrs Mary Were of Chalfont St Giles in Buckinghamshire earned her nickname St Francis by demonstrating her ability with sick animals. On one occasion she healed a pigeon's broken leg with a surgical boot made out of cork. She also set a frog's leg with a matchstick, but her real *pièce de résistance* was to fit a wooden leg on to a duck after its own had been severed in an accident.

*   *   *

To reassure perturbed pet-owners away on holiday, some American boarding kennels send them postcards complete with their pets' paw print signature.

*   *   *

In 1981, Britain's vets expressed concern at the

number of inebriated animals that they were having to treat. Pub dogs with hangovers and parrots with cirrhosis of the liver were becoming part of the vets' workload, as owners persuaded pets to perform party tricks. One such pet was Hercules the wrestling bear, who weighed in at 54 stone. By day, Hercules would sup gallons of ale, but by night he turned to the more exotic and would down a bottle of advocaat! Another case was that of Jason the tabby cat, who resided at a pub in Sevenoaks, Kent. Turning up his whiskers at the usual saucer of milk, Jason preferred to lap up Snowballs.

*　　　*　　　*

In the 1980s, scientists in America claimed they were not far off creating a new super-race of pets. Dr Joseph Debolt from the University of Central Michigan said excitedly that he was only 'a few steps away' from breeding cats and dogs that could walk on their hind legs and use their paws as hands. Dr Joe also thought that such pets could be fitted with voice-boxes and taught how to talk. Another idea was to raise bears capable of being security guards. Boston psychologist Dr George Fournier even went as far as to say that pigeons would make ideal quality-control workers for use in industry. As radical as these ideas sound, the US Navy took them seriously, and made investigations into using sharks as deterrents against military frogmen planning to sabotage US ships.

*   *   *

In 1983, a loan-a-pet scheme was set up by a group of doctors, vets and social workers in conjunction with the RSPCA. The idea was that suitable pets would be loaned to the lonely, depressed and mentally ill. Pensioners living alone, who were unable to keep pets because of accommodation restrictions, could have the companionship of a dog or cat for a few hours each day. Similar schemes had already proved to be successful in the States. Spending time with pets has shown to be beneficial in the recovery of depressed patients. What it does to the pets themselves is anyone's guess.

*   *   *

In 1992 in Japan, mobile crematorium units could be called to the scene of a pet's death. These mobile vans were specially built to make sure that no telltale pall of smoke escaped into the atmosphere. The vans were also marked discreetly, so that no one had to suffer the embarrassment of everyone knowing that they were actually having their late pet cremated in the street. The van contained a plain platform for the coffin which was flanked by a border of flowers. Taped Buddhist songs could also be played, in order to set the right tone for the occasion. In fact, everything had been considered. The burning process was carefully set at a temperature which would leave the pet's bones intact. Takayuki Sato, head of the Tokyo branch of the mobile crematorium company, explained: 'If people just send their pet off somewhere for cremation they're left with an unsettled feeling. If they can actually see it with their own eyes and then put the bones in a jar, they feel extremely satisfied.'

*   *   *

In his 1967 book, *Psychic Pets*, Joseph Wylder told of the horse called Lady Wonder who learned how to type. The filly answered questions by touching keys which were specially adapted large rubber pads with her muzzle.

Lady Wonder is reputedly to have picked out winners in horse races and even to have predicted Harry Truman's election victory in 1948. So convinced were some Americans that Lady Wonder was, in fact, a genius that they actually paid to ask her questions.